Out of The Depths

Hope in Times of Suffering

Theological Resources in Times of Persecution

An Anglican Contribution to Ecumenical Engagement

By the Anglican Inter Faith Network

Published by the Anglican Consultative Council
16 Tavistock Crescent
London W11 1AP, UK
ISBN 978-1-911007-06-7

 Set in Adobe Caslon Pro 12/18.

Contents

Foreword by Archbishop Mouneer Hanna Anis

Every day we hear of painful incidents of persecutions in many different parts of the world. There is no doubt that persecutions of our brothers and sisters, members of the Body of Christ, break our heart and bring up the question: how can we respond to this?

St Paul helps us to find the answer to this question in his words 'Bless those who persecute you; bless and do not curse', 'Do not repay anyone evil for evil, but take thought for what is noble in the sight of all' (Rom 12.14, 17).

I found *Out of the Depths* to be a wonderful resource for the Church worldwide as she tries to respond to those who suffer. I highly recommend it.

The Most Revd Dr Mouneer Hanna Anis

Archbishop of Episcopal/Anglican Diocese of Egypt with North Africa and the Horn of Africa

Commendation by Archbishop Justin Welby

At a crucial time in world history, when religious persecution and violence are on the rise, both God's world and Christ's body, the Church, face enormous pain and suffering. We are encouraged, through engaging with this welcome resource, to renew our commitment to prayer, Scripture, reason, and tradition and to be reminded of the true hope in Jesus Christ from whom all comfort, courage, and peace can be found. I commend this timely contribution from the Anglican Inter Faith Network as it seeks to benefit all Christian traditions in our understanding of the faith in Christ which unites and upholds us.

The Most Revd & Rt Hon. Justin Welby

Archbishop of Canterbury

1 Introduction

i Settings: Global, Ecumenical, and Anglican

We are living in an unprecedented time of religious persecution and martyrdom in the modern world. There were more recognized martyrs in the twentieth century than in the whole of previous Christian history. There are some books on the demography and phenomenology of persecution, but currently a lack of theological resources to help those who are undergoing persecution.

'Out of the depths I cry to you, O Lord' is the beginning of Psalm 130.1. Facing the threat of being overwhelmed by the waters of chaos, the Psalmist cries out for help from the depths of his heart.

Our title, 'Out of the Depths – Hope in Times of Suffering', draws on that Psalm and also on Psalm 42.7:

> *Deep calls to deep at the thunder of your cataracts;*
> *all your waves and your billows have gone over me.*

The Psalmist again uses the image of water for being pounded in the midst of trouble and woe, and cries out for help.

We are conscious of our ecumenical context. Three occasions were of particular importance in 2015: the fiftieth anniversary of *Dignitatis Humanae*, the decree on Religious Freedom of Vatican II, December 1965; the consultation on persecution in November 2015, in Tirana, Albania, organized by the Global Christian Forum, which gathered representatives of all the major streams in World Christianity; and the centenary of the Armenian Genocide.

The Inter Faith Network of the Anglican Communion has published two theological resources so far: *Generous Love: The Truth of the Gospel and the Call to Dialogue* (written in 2008) and *Land of Promise? An Anglican Exploration of Christian Attitudes to the Holy Land* (written in 2012). This book is the third in our series, after another four years.

It was written for the Anglican Consultative Council's sixteenth meeting in Lusaka, Zambia, in April 2016, and we pray that it will be a resource for Christians of all traditions, for those who are under persecution and also for those who support them.

ii Methodology

The Virginia Report (Anglican Consultative Council, 1997) of the Inter-Anglican Theological and Doctrinal Commission stated:

Anglicans are held together by the characteristic way in which they use Scripture, tradition and reason in discerning afresh the mind of Christ for the Church in each generation. This was well described in the Report of the Pastoral and Dogmatic Concerns section of Lambeth 1988. (para 3.5)

Anglicans affirm the sovereign authority of the Holy Scriptures as the medium through which God by the Spirit communicates his word in the Church and thus enables people to respond with understanding and faith. The Scriptures are 'uniquely inspired witness to divine revelation', and 'the primary norm for Christian faith and life'. (para 3.6)

The Scriptures, however, must be translated, read, and understood, and their meaning must be grasped through a continuing process of interpretation. Since the seventeenth century Anglicans have held Scripture is to be understood and read in the light afforded by the contexts of 'tradition' and 'reason'. (para 3.7)

Generous Love: The Truth of the Gospel and the Call to Dialogue (Anglican Consultative Council, 2008) also referred to this interplay:

> *Anglicans hold that Scripture is to be interpreted in the light of tradition and reason, meaning by these an appeal respectively to the mind of the Church as that develops and to the mind of the cultures in which the Church participates. Tradition and reason are shaped by the lived experiences of Christians in their double contexts of Church and society, and they are inseparable as are those contexts. (p. 7)*

In this document, we resonate with this methodology by beginning with prayer, reflecting on our contexts, studying the Scriptures, Tradition, and Reason and ending with worship.

Chapter 1 Introduction, begins with prayer, as well as some basic definitions.

Chapter 2 outlines our global context, through life studies which reflect the input and conversations we have had with Christians from India, Malaysia, Nigeria, Sweden, Syria and the USA.

Chapter 3 elucidates the Scriptures on our theme, drawing out personal and corporate insights.

Chapter 4 describes Tradition: how diverse theologies have resourced Christians under pressure through the centuries.

Chapter 5 expounds the meaning of Reason in the contemporary context, including considering how people of other faiths have drawn on their own theological resources.

Chapter 6 focuses upon worship.

iii Prayer

The prayer which Jesus taught his disciples is nourishing as a theological resource.

This is Matthew's version in the Sermon on the Mount (Mt 6.9–13):

Our Father in heaven,
hallowed be your name.
Your kingdom come.
Your will be done,
on earth as it is in heaven.
Give us this day our daily bread.
And forgive us our debts,
as we also have forgiven our debtors.
And do not bring us to the time of trial,
but rescue us from the evil one.

Jesus shares his unique address to God as Father with his disciples, thus underlining their membership of the family, through him. God's name is often besmirched when his people are persecuted, and here they pray for it to be 'hallowed'.

Prayer for the fuller coming of the God's rule is explored further in the next request, 'Your will be done, on earth as it is in heaven.' The two go together, as later on in this chapter: 'strive first for the kingdom of God and his righteousness' (Mt 6.33).

Joachim Jeremias, the Lutheran scholar of Aramaic and New Testament Studies, wrote some helpful comments on the Lord's Prayer. He interpreted the original Aramaic of 'Give us this day our daily bread' as:

> *Tomorrow's bread, give us today.*

He elucidated this further as:

> *Now, here and now, today, give us the bread of life in the midst of our sorry existence.*

In 'forgive us our debts, as we also have forgiven our debtors' we see that this prayer is shaped to heal relationships, even the starkest of oppressive relationships. The surprise about this petition for forgiveness is that God is boldly asked to be imitators of us, rather than the usual other way round, though obviously our forgiveness is based on his prior forgiveness. This may be the hardest of the petitions for those under persecution. The comment of Jesus, following his prayer in Matthew's gospel, also mentions forgiveness (vv. 14–15) and thus underlines its centrality in the prayer.

The Litany in *The Book of Common Prayer* has this significant petition:

> *That it may please thee to forgive our enemies, persecutors, and slanderers, and to turn their hearts.*

Jeremias suggested that 'do not bring us to the time of trial' was:

> *a request for preservation from succumbing to the eschatological trial. Jesus' disciples are therefore praying, at the end of the Lord's Prayer, for protection against apostasy … Grant us one thing, preserve us from going wrong.*[1]

The plaintive cry of the heart to be delivered from evil, or the evil one, has echoed throughout the centuries of persecution.

Mark does not have the Lord's Prayer in his gospel but it is intriguingly echoed in the Garden of Gethsemane (Mk 14). Having shared their last *daily bread* at the Last Supper (vv. 22–25), Jesus mentions the *kingdom*: 'Truly I tell you, I will never again drink of the fruit of the vine until that day when I drink it new in the kingdom

1 Joachim Jeremias, *New Testament Theology*, vol. I (London: SCM, 1971), pp. 199–201.

of God' (v. 25) and then states that Peter will *fall into temptation* under pressure (vv. 26–31). In the garden, Jesus cries '*Abba*', submits to his father's *will* (v. 36), and then scolds Simon Peter, 'Keep awake and pray that you may not come into the *time of trial*' (v. 38).

iv Spectrum of Persecution

A spectrum of persecution may be delineated, from 'squeeze' to 'smash'. These stages may be seen as:

- 'Harassment', where people have subtle consistent pressure put upon them.
- 'Subjugation', where they are kept down, as a lower class in law.
- 'Persecution', where they are physically and violently attacked, by individuals or the State.
- 'Martyrdom', where they are killed for their faith or for standing for justice. The primary etymological meaning is one of 'witness', which is the Spirit-led response of faith to

extreme persecution. In this sense, which is stressed by Orthodox Christians, it stands outside any spectrum of human hostility, as a gift of grace.

- 'Annihilation', where whole peoples are wiped out.
- 'Obliteration', where the original existence of the annihilated peoples is denied, or they are 'airbrushed' out of the picture, such as the destruction of Armenian churches and artefacts in Turkey, denial of the Holocaust (or Shoah), and the destruction of churches by Daesh.[2]

This book seeks to provide 'theological resources in times of persecution', and the latter word is expansive in both directions along the spectrum from the centre.

2 Sometimes referred to as IS (Islamic State) or ISIL (Islamic State of Iraq and the Levant) or ISIS (Islamic State of Iraq and al-Sham), but it is not a state and is not seen by most Muslims as being Islamic.

2 Global Context

This chapter includes six current life studies and two historical stories of religious persecution that feed into a reflection upon being part of a suffering Body.

Life Studies from Asia, Middle East and Africa

The first four life studies come from individual Anglicans in Malaysia, Syria, and Nigeria and from United Churches in India. The life studies were shared with the writers in November 2014. Although what follows has been edited, the words, sentiments, and conclusions are those shared by these individuals from these four countries.

i Malaysia

Although Malaysia had traditionally had an inclusive approach to religions, in 2001 the Malaysian government declared that Islam was the state religion. After race riots, there was a power struggle between different Islamic parties which moved thinking away from the previous inclusive approach and laws were introduced that marginalized minorities.

Currently Christians cannot use the word Allah for God. At the grass-roots level, communities are encouraged to introduce Sharia. It is not just the non-Islamic minorities that feel persecuted, but also some of the more liberal Muslims. This has led to migration from the country; as the more open and academic Muslims have left the situation has become more extreme.

The situation is being driven by identity, and a quest for meaning. For ethnic Malays, Islam gives them this security. They feel that Indians have India, Chinese have China, and Westerners have the West, but Malays only have Malaysia! In a digital era young people are impacted by outside influences, and Malaysian Christians are concerned by the extreme Islamic views in the Middle East.

Christians look towards the eschatological hope in Christ; until then they live with that hope and try to engage positively, rather than negatively. Of course, some Christians are keen to leave and 'feel called' to minister elsewhere!

Malaysian Christians are unashamedly living by gospel values and living out their faith. Although many Christians elsewhere say that Islam is a peaceful religion this doesn't tie in with Malaysia's experience and it doesn't sound as if such Christians know about Islam in the Malaysian situation; they need to acknowledge the pain of Malaysian Christians. Malaysian Christians want to see what these Christians are doing in the way of policies. Malaysian Christians do not believe in a prosperity gospel but are aware that Christians will suffer for gospel values. They feel that there is confusion and a sense of chaos within the Anglican Communion, related to the sexuality issue, as to what the world says and what the Bible says. Malaysian Christians believe that Anglicans should first address what is happening within the Anglican Communion, then what is happening in their own countries. At this time of suffering, Malaysian Christians want narratives about what is happening that can encourage rather than discourage them.

ii India

In some places churches are being destroyed by the majority Hindu community despite the congregations feeling that they have done nothing to provoke such action. Elsewhere some Christian property is being annexed by RSS,[3] and it is very difficult to open new churches.

There are examples of churches being destroyed after missionaries, from other parts of India, have demonized Hinduism either through the testimonies of recent converts or through distributing pamphlets that demonize Hindu gods. The missionaries doing this then leave the area and don't suffer any consequences themselves. There can also be a reaction against perceived inducements for people to convert to Christianity; often there might be a narrow divide between Christian service, and respect for Christian service, and a material inducement to become a Christian.

3 Rashtriya Swayamsevak Sangh, a Hindu nationalist non-government organization.

In some places persecution is influenced by population explosion and economics; minorities are blamed for the economic impact and are persecuted. People enjoy the financial gains of a market economy, but fear the values that go with it.

Dalits[4] comprise 17 per cent of India's population and tribal people 8 per cent, but Dalits and tribal people together comprise 60 per cent or more of Christians in the south and more than 80 per cent of Christians in the north. This means that often it is difficult to say whether Christians are suffering for their faith or for their place within the caste system. The Indian constitution protects minorities but, with political changes, it must be questioned whether this can be sustained in the next five to ten years.

4 This is the self-chosen political name of the castes in India that were formerly considered to be 'untouchable' within the Hindu Varna system. The word 'Dalit' means 'oppressed' in Hindi and Marathi.

In one area there was a situation where tribal peoples killed a Hindu leader leading to a conflict between the tribal peoples and the caste people with Christians being killed as ‘collateral damage’, rather than as part of any religious persecution.

There are also long-term missionaries dedicated to the area and work whose theology is such that they expect to be persecuted for their witness, so they have acted knowing that their actions are likely to bring about persecution upon themselves.

Having said this, most Hindus, as always, are living in close proximity, and in mutual respect, to Christians and share much, not least in education and other ways. Such majority Hindus are deeply embarrassed by the scapegoating of Christians; this is particularly true in the south, where there are many Christians.

iii Syria

Syria is facing a massive human tragedy; by November 2014 300,000 lives had been lost and 5–6 million people displaced [sources suggest that an additional 55,000 were killed in 2015, and by March 2016 figures suggest 6.5 million internally displaced and 3 million in neighbouring countries]. Thousands of Christians are being killed and Christian and Alawi women are being sold in markets. The level of suffering in the Middle East is similar to that inflicted in 1259–60 by Genghis Khan. Young people, between 17 and 23, are sharing absolute despair and saying, 'Are you asking us to stay and die?' The response is 'If it is die or leave, then leave. If it is to stay in difficult circumstances, then stay.' People are finding ways to stay, and paying a tax (in gold) to stay is a way of not converting.

What was suffered under ISIS (Daesh) was horrible, but Muslim neighbours betraying Christians to ISIS was worse. The Nazarene sign, meaning a follower of Jesus of Nazareth, was put on houses. This meant the occupier could be killed and property taken; there is the need to start building trust again. There is the need for a humanitarian response but awareness of the real issues as well.

It is my understanding that the rise of Islamic fundamentalism is still a taboo subject in the West who speak of jihadis, rather than Muslims, as it is not politically correct to connect jihadis to Islam. There is the need to engage with the current persecution by Muslims. The Church in the West has failed to respond adequately to the suffering of Christians in the Middle East. The West has also turned a blind eye to the flow of jihadis to Syria through Turkey.

There has been no serious and persistent persecution of Christians in the Western world for many centuries, so there is an absence of a theology of persecution and suffering for faith. Western Christianity has a habit of seeing Christianity as being a Western phenomenon; there is no concept of Middle Eastern culture when we reflect theologically. Most Protestant theology taught in the Middle East is Western, ignoring the Middle Eastern heritage. Eastern Christians are used to persecution, but not at this current level.

Martyrdom is not seeking death for the sake of Christ; martyrdom is seeking life. But if asked to carry the cross to death, we need to be obedient. The early Church persecution was by pagans, but during the Crusades Christian suffering was caused by Western Christians. Eastern Christians have been invisible to the West. Archbishop Rowan said, 'If you want to learn about Christian martyrdom go to the Middle East, not the history books.'

Three theological principles:

- Obedience to the Lord – carrying your cross might be literal;
- Hope – the world should see the hope in us and wonder about that hope. The challenge of having, or not having, hope in the midst of persecution;
- Blessing – 'Blessed are those who are persecuted for righteousness' sake, and those persecuted for my name.' We become a blessing in society and spread blessings; an example has been closer ecumenical relationships in Middle East than before.

iv Nigeria

In northern Nigeria, even outside the Boko Haram areas you can't get land for a church if you ask for it. Christians try to buy land for other purposes and then build a church on it. The church is then demolished and this is seen as persecution.

The north-east, where Boko Haram is particularly active, is 96 per cent Muslim, a similar percentage to Somalia. So why do Boko Haram see the need for further Islamization? The Sultan says that Boko Haram is not Islam, but this not being heard by the Christians in the south of Nigeria.

Northern Nigeria had 11 million Muslims and 400,000 Christians in 1958. An increased Christian population in the southern part of the north has seen tensions rise. Only 3 per cent of those in the northern part of the north are indigenous Christians; Christians from the southern part of northern Nigeria have sometimes moved to the northern part. Some Pentecostals are causing problems, by trying to convert Muslims without first having an existing relationship with them.

The theological mind-set is very Western and the leadership has often been trained in the UK or US. If there is no persecution then our belief in Christ is questionable. We are still evolving an African theological understanding. Africa is very diverse: east–west; north–south; central; Ghanaian; Nigerian. There are huge differences within Nigeria. The West is very offensive in trying to stereotype Africans or even Nigerians; understanding the context is very important.

In Africa there is often hatred between the different religious communities. In Nigeria, an exception has been the Yoruba, who have taken on board cooperation and who do relate and will go to mosques and churches with family members. Sadly the Yoruba are picking up on tensions from elsewhere. Relationships have been very bad, even in majority Christian or majority Islam countries relationships are bad, because of the lack of theological understanding.

Is the African able to separate Christianity from tribe? As a Christian and a Nigerian, am I a Christian Nigerian or a Nigerian Christian? Is the African Christian able to accept common beliefs across Bible and Qur'ān? The Pentecostals refuse to do this, but we need to have some agreement before we can tackle Africa's problems. Pentecostals would also say that Allah is not God.

Nigeria is a microcosm of Africa. What is the African biblical understanding of persecution? Africans see themselves as brothers and sisters who care for each other across tribal boundaries; but this has been lost among Christians.

Life Studies from Europe and North America

As mentioned in the above narrative from Syria, 'There has been no serious and persistent persecution of Christians in the Western world for many centuries.' However, we have included life studies from the USA and the Church in Sweden.[5] We are aware that these stories of persecution from the USA and Sweden are at a very different level from that described within the other narratives, but believe that they are representative of Western countries and that this material helps shape the understanding of persecution, and the theology of persecution, of many Christians in the West.

Both life studies were shared with the writers in

5 The Church of Sweden is, like other Lutheran churches in the Nordic and Baltic countries, linked in the Porvoo Communion with British and Irish Anglican Churches in a relationship of full intercommunion and interchangeability of ministries.

November 2014, but the Swedish story was updated a year later. Again, although what follows has been edited, the words, sentiments, and conclusions are those shared by these individuals from these two countries.

v Sweden

If Christians can be said to be subjected to any form of persecution in Sweden, it is a question of very mild forms of harassment. Jews and Muslims are worse off, as there is widespread antisemitism and Islamophobia in society; especially Muslim women who wear a headscarf are often subjected to harassment, sometimes in a violent physical form.

If you are religious at all in Sweden, many people tend to think that you are a bit daft. This will mean that children can be bullied at school if they are openly Christian, not only by their peers, but sometimes even by teachers. This, however, is slowly changing as more children with an immigrant background are proud to be Muslims or Christians, and the schools realize that they have to take religion more seriously.

As long as religion is a case of ideas, it is protected by the laws of freedom of speech. There have been two instances where a few years ago a pastor and recently an imam were brought to court for comparing homosexuality to a disease, but were acquitted. Even though their opinions went counter to Swedish legislation and the general opinion, they were allowed to express them.

A post-Protestant, secular society like Sweden has, however, difficulties understanding that religion can also be expressed in dressing and eating. While halal slaughter, where the animal is sedated before it is killed, is allowed, Jewish kosher slaughter, where the animal cannot be sedated, is not allowed. Animal rights have taken precedence over religious rights. Circumcision of boys is allowed, but calls for making it unlawful have been raised several times lately. Children's rights to bodily autonomy are more important than religious rights, is the argument put forward in favour of legislation.

A midwife cannot claim that because of her Christian faith she cannot assist at abortions. A Muslim nurse cannot claim that she must have long sleeves. Workplace rules and hygiene take precedence before religious considerations.

It is often hard to distinguish harassment on religious grounds from xenophobia. 'Muslim' has become a code word for 'immigrant' in right-wing extremism. The Muslim is the 'ultimate other'.

When harassment happens, it is often between or within religious groups. A special Swedish feature is the great number of Christians from the Middle East, who carry persecution baggage with them; they are often very hostile to Muslims. This is a dilemma for indigenous Swedish Christians, especially the Church of Sweden, who want to cultivate good relations with both groups. Much antisemitism comes from Muslims with roots in the Middle East.

Another case is the critique directed at Christians who engage publicly in interfaith dialogue, especially Christian–Muslim dialogue. This comes particularly from other Christians, often in liaison with right-wing activists. This critique can indeed take the form of rather vile harassment on social media, as well as email and phone calls of a threatening nature. At the moment this appears to be a growing problem that might hamper the development of interfaith dialogue.

vi North America

In 2013, there were 115 attacks on places of worship and 75 fatalities. These have included attacks on synagogues by neo-Nazis, which have also killed non-Jews.

There are 'freedom of speech' demonstrations at the funerals of some homosexuals in the armed forces and also at some family planning clinics which include abortion among their services. Some opposition by people to the 'Obamacare' health care reforms was because it includes family planning.

This persecution in the US is from the extreme right, often some of the Christian religious right. These acts are classified as hate crimes and are prosecuted. Secularism is seen as a bad thing.

Although the US considers itself the most religious country in the world, I believe that theological literacy can be poor, and that the persecution referred to above comes out of a distortion of a particular Christian theology. On a positive note, acts of persecution can often bring people and communities together and lead to some sense of healing.

Historical Stories

The following two historical stories consider some of the issues related to surviving persecution.

vii Third-Century Carthage, North Africa

In AD 250, the Roman authorities demanded that all citizens should sacrifice to pagan gods; Christian bishops were particularly targeted with the threat of execution. Shortly before this, Cyprian had been appointed as Bishop of Carthage. This choice was controversial: welcomed by the poor, but opposed by many of the senior clergy who felt that his rise to this position had been too rapid. Rather than face potential execution, Cyprian fled. He explained that it was important for the bishop, as shepherd, to remain alive and be able to lead his people from a distance and that this was what God willed. He also saw precedents in the lives of some of the apostles. Those opposed to his appointment as bishop condemned him as a coward.

During the subsequent persecution, many Christians either, under the threat of persecution, signed certificates to say that they had sacrificed to pagan gods or, in response to persecution, torture, confiscation of property or death, did actually sacrifice. From a distance, Cyprian demanded public penance before such Christians were re-admitted to the Church. Some of those presbyters who had opposed Cyprian's appointment as bishop ignored his authority and allowed these Christians back easily, with minimal penance.

Schism occurred when those presbyters who were opposed to Cyprian elected Fortunatus as bishop in opposition to Cyprian. There was a similar schism in Rome at this time, when Novatian, who took a firmer stand than Cyprian and refused absolution to any Christians who had sacrificed to Roman gods, was elected Bishop of Rome in opposition to Cornelius. The Novatianists then also appointed Maximus, a rival bishop of their own, as a third bishop in Carthage. Cyprian, insisting upon public penance, was now seen as a moderating influence between these other two positions of either not requiring penance or refusing any absolution.

viii Seventeenth-Century Japan

Following the Shimabara rebellion of 1638, in order to eradicate Christianity, the whole population of Japan were required to register at a family temple and be issued with a temple certificate to confirm that they were not

Christians. To achieve this, they had to take part in an annual rite entitled 'ebumi' (image trampling), in which they had to trample upon Christian imagery. To encourage apostasy, rather than martyrdom, some very long and lingering forms of death had been devised for those who confessed Christianity and refused ebumi.

To avoid death and the wiping out of Christianity, many Christian communities chose ebumi followed by prayers of confession. Some communities took along spare straw sandals for this act of desecration, and as soon as possible changed out of these soiled sandals, burnt them, added water to the ash, and drank this mixture as an act of penance.

From this period, there also survive several artefacts which present initially as ordinary Buddhist, Shinto, or folk religious objects, but which closer inspection reveals to conceal Christian devotional aids, e.g. a cross appears when light is shone through a Shinto sacred mirror, a crucifix is carved into the back of a sitting statue of the Buddha, the Virgin Mary is depicted in the form of the bodhisattva of compassion Kannon.

Being Part of a Suffering Body

Events in Paris in January 2015 had parallels with the film *Spartacus*. Spartacus led a failed rebellion against the Romans in the first century BC. To subject Spartacus to a particularly brutal death the Romans ask their captives to identify him. In turn, each captive responds, 'I am Spartacus', and each is crucified. The crucifixions and sense of belonging to, and suffering for, something greater than self contain strong Christian imagery.

On 7 January 2015 two armed Islamists attacked the offices of *Charlie Hebdo*. This secular magazine was famous for publishing blasphemous articles and cartoons mocking Christian and political views, and leaders, as well as Islam and the Prophet. After killing two police officers, one a Muslim named Ahmed Merabet, the terrorists entered the building and executed ten of the magazine staff. As the police sought, and eventually located, the killers, another Islamist terrorist, in an attempt to bargain for the freedom of the original terrorists, took hostages in a Jewish supermarket, killing four Jewish people.

The events led to a global response, initially on social networks and then in demonstrations of solidarity with those who had been killed, culminating in a march in Paris, including not only Western leaders but leaders from Saudi Arabia, Palestine, and Israel. The main social network phrase, and the message on the banners at the marches, was *Je suis Charlie* – 'I am Charlie'. Small minorities identified with two other slogans on social media and at marches. Again, echoing the phrase 'I am Spartacus', these slogans were:

Je suis Ahmed – I am not Charlie, I am Ahmed the dead cop. Charlie ridiculed my faith and culture and I died defending his right to do so.

Je suis Juif – I am Jewish.

In the Syrian life study above, mention is made of the Nazarene sign identifying Christians. Although not making the headlines as much as the three '*Je suis*' statements, a number of Christians, to show solidarity with persecuted Christians in Syria and Iraq, started to use this sign in their Facebook profiles.

These recent events help raise the question of our own identity. Do we identify with our national cultural world-view, be that the liberal Western world-view defined by *Je suis Charlie* or another national world-view? Do we identify with *Je suis Ahmed*, and try to hold together the ambiguities of being a good citizen of our state with our faith identity? Do we identify with *Je suis Juif* or the Nazarene sign, and identify with a persecuted minority? After the killings, the publication of the next edition of *Charlie Hebdo* (by secularists who mock Christianity as much as they mock Islam) led to attacks by Islamists on forty-five churches in the former French colony of Niger, with ten people killed.

What is your identity? In the Nigerian narrative, the narrator asks if he is a Christian Nigerian or a Nigerian

Christian. Your deepest sense of belonging might be because of faith or denomination, but it might be shaped by national or regional culture, tribe, ethnicity, or socio-political identity. For some, all of these will coincide. Although this leads to a deep sense of belonging, with others who share this identity, it can become harder to determine which factors in their identity are dominant; is it really faith, or is it one or more of the other factors that are determining how faith is understood and lived out? As was asked in the life study from India, were people being persecuted because they were Christians, or because they were Dalit or tribal people?

The growth of religious fundamentalisms, as well as secularism, is the common background to the six life studies; this growth means that we all are likely to become increasingly aware of the distinctive world-view that our own faith affirms, and the Japanese narrative reminds us that if we are to survive as a religious minority there can also be the risk of syncretism. Although we are seeking a distinctive Christian perspective, this will be shaped by our own context. This is not a new phenomenon and was an issue that Paul addressed.

Paul acknowledges the diversity and creative tension within the Body of Christ, stating that 'you who once were far off have been brought near by the blood of Christ. For he is our peace; in his flesh he has made both groups into one and has broken down the dividing wall' (Eph 2.13–14) and 'In him the whole structure is joined together and grows into a holy temple in the Lord; in whom you also are built together spiritually into a dwelling-place for God' (Eph 2.21–22). Professor Andrew Walls argues that if Christ is the Lord of the whole world 'the church must be diverse because humanity is diverse; it must be one because Christ is one.'[6] Paul also reminds us of our mutual interdependence within the Body of Christ (1 Cor 12.12–21) and that 'If one member suffers, all suffer together with it' (1 Cor 12.26).

Anglicans try to make this sense of belonging to the one body real in different ways: formally through four Instruments of Communion;[7] through informal relationships;[8] through prayer.[9] Despite this, Christians who suffer can sometimes feel that other parts of the Body not only don't help, but can exacerbate the suffering. Stories of insensitive evangelism and Qur'ān burning

---

6 Andrew Walls, The Ephesian Moment, published 2002, www.anglicancommunion.org/listening/book_resources/docs/ephesian_moment.pdf.

7 The Lambeth Conference, the Anglican Consultative Council, the Primates' Meeting, and the Archbishop of Canterbury. See www.anglicancommunion.org/communion/index.cfm.

8 Such as Companion Links; see www.anglicancommunion.org/community/church-links.aspx. For the Mothers' Union and other mission agencies and networks, see www.anglicancommunion.org/networks/index.cfm.

9 See www.anglicancommunion.org/acp/.

are a reminder that the actions of some Christians can provoke the persecution of other Christians. Within cultures where all are considered to be religious, rather than secular, this situation is aggravated by the perception, as in the reference to *Charlie Hebdo* and church burning in Niger, that Western values are Christian rather than secular.

The other aggravating issue is the perception, when you are suffering for taking a Christian stand, that other Christians are not only not taking a stand, but going along with their local cultural values, rather than Christian values. Also, when another faith community doesn't let you build a Christian place of worship it is difficult to hear that Christians in another part of the world appear to have more concern for that same faith community than for their fellow Christians in your country.

As the voices from Malaysia and Syria made clear, a very real additional source of pain is the perception that many Western Christians have rejected Christian values and gone along with Western liberal cultural values on issues of sexuality. These Western Christians would, in turn, respond that they believe that this is the appropriate biblical understanding within their own culture and context. The Swedish and American life studies remind us that people undergo persecution because of their sexuality or for belonging to a non-Christian faith. It is then easy to argue that authentic Christian mission in such a culture and context requires standing up for these persecuted groups.

Persecution in third-century Carthage led to schism, and our current life studies show how persecution makes theological differences more obvious, and more painful. In the farewell discourses in John's gospel, Jesus warns his followers that the world is likely to hate them (Jn 15.18), and compares their inter-connectedness to a vine (Jn 15); he reminds them of the importance of loving each other (Jn 13.34), and his prayer is that they should be one (Jn 17.21).

Jesus asks his disciples, 'who do people say that I am?' (Mt 16.13, Mk 8.29, Lk 9.18). Having answered that question, in the light of the suffering and persecution of other Christians, and our part in the Body of Christ, we each need to ask the question 'who do people say that I am?' of ourselves. What is our own identity as part of the suffering Body of Christ?

The answer is unlikely to be one that can be summed up with a simple 'I am ...' or *Je suis ...* ' but should help us shape our listening, our understanding, our compassion, our words, our prayers and petitions, and our actions and interactions as part of the Body of Christ.

Reflection and Response

A For each of the life studies i–vi, reflect upon the following questions:

1. Are there any signs of hope in this life study?
2. Has there been any provocation, and if so, by whom?
3. What options were open to those being persecuted? Is there a strategy for survival?
4. In what way do those persecuted feel that they are part of the Body of Christ?
5. In what way, in response to the life study, do you feel part of the Body of Christ?
6. What new theological insights have you gained from this life study?
7. What responses does this life study suggest for your own life?

B In the light of the two historical stories, vii and viii, consider, where relevant, how these questions apply to life studies i–vi and other current examples of persecution:

1. May Christian leaders expect to be dealt with more harshly than other Christians?
2. Is flight sometimes an appropriate action for those for whom it is possible?
3. Should those who compromise their faith be re-admitted to the church or not, and, if so, what penance is required?
4. What are the risks of syncretism for those involved in secret worship within another faith environment?
5. Are the risks of schism increased during times of trial?
6. Is schism based upon doctrinal issues more likely when broken relationships or cultural differences already exist?

C Being part of the suffering body

1. How does being part of the suffering Body of Christ impact upon your sense of identity and your sense of belonging?
2. Who do people say that you are? Are you primarily identified by your nationality, culture, ethnicity, socio-political group or your faith?
3. Who are the persecuted in your context, and what does a Christian witness with respect to their suffering require of you?

D Response

1. Write a prayer of praise to thank God for signs of hope, purpose, and faithfulness in situations of persecution.
2. With regard to persecution, attitudes to the persecuted, or failure to respond as part of the Body of Christ, what do you need to repent of, either personally or on behalf of your nation or church?
3. Are there any actions, with regard to gaining further information, prayer, or advocacy, that you feel called to take?

3 Scripture

Old Testament

Many scholars consider that Genesis chapter 1 was written in the context of persecution. The leaders of the Jews were in exile in Babylon. The 'Priestly Writer' took the Babylonian myths of creation, with their multiple gods, and transformed them radically into a powerful statement that the true God, worshipped by the Jews, was the God of the whole universe: not just the God of the land promised to Abraham, Isaac, and Jacob, but the God of the whole universe.

This portrayal of the immensity and eternity of God gave hope in the midst of their depths in Babylon.

These insights have given heart to countless people across the centuries and the globe, for example concerning the persecution of black people under the apartheid regime of South Africa.

Human beings are made in the image of God (Gen 1.27). If you persecute the image, you attack the Original.

In Genesis chapter 4, Cain, the agriculturalist, persecuted his brother Abel, the pastoralist. Tensions between brothers and these 'types of farmers' are perennial. After the murder, the Lord said, 'Listen; your brother's blood is crying out to me from the ground!' (Gen 4.10). If you murder, God hears.

Family rivalry continued, in Genesis 16 and 17, in the relationship between Sarai (Abraham's wife and the mother of Isaac, the son of promise) and Hagar (Sarai's Egyptian slave-girl and the mother of Ishmael). Abraham sent Hagar and Ishmael into the wilderness but God, who fulfilled his promise through Isaac, also protected Hagar and Ishmael (Gen 21). If you drive people out, God is still with them.

Sibling rivalry continued between the sons of Isaac, Jacob and Esau (Gen 25–33), with their reversal of fortunes, threat of war, and eventual reconciliation, and between the sons of Jacob, who persecuted their provocatively proud brother, Joseph (Gen 37–45). They sold him into slavery in Egypt, but God sent him before them to preserve their lives (Gen 45). If you persecute, God sometimes preserves even you, the persecutor.

In the book of Exodus, we see that when rulers change, flourishing can turn to hardship. The new Pharaoh hated the foreigners in his midst, the Israelites, because of their increasing numbers. He made them slaves and ordered the killing of their baby boys (Ex 1). 'God heard their groaning, and God remembered his covenant with Abraham, Isaac, and Jacob' (Ex 2.24). If you are oppressed, God hears and remembers.

The Lord liberated his people from Egypt, by the sheer power of the plagues (Ex 7–12). He took sides, for his people and against the oppressive Egyptians. He gave birth in blood to a nation through the Red Sea (Ex 14).

The conquest of Canaan, the Promised Land, by the Israelites could be seen, from the perspective of the native tribes, as persecution: the Hebrew Scriptures, in one strand, present the conquest as part of God's plan. The slaughter of the Amalekites was different from the conquest of the six nations, because the Amalekites were nomads who attacked those who were feeble among the Israelites in the Sinai desert (Ex 17 and Deut 25), and continued to be a threat throughout Israelite history. In Jewish and Rabbinic scholarship over the years, these texts referring to the Amalekites have been agonized over, in discussion and comment, and ways have been found to remove their apparent genocidal nature.

Again, family rivalry surfaces in the narratives of David, who was attacked by his son Absalom and forced to flee. However, when his son met his grisly end, David was devastated in grief (2 Sam 15–18). If you are oppressed, you can still grieve at the demise of your oppressor, especially if you are related.

The whole Psalter, Jesus' prayer book, is the quintessential theological resource for people under pressure: 'Out of the depths I cry to you, O Lord' (Ps 130.1). We read Psalms of communal lament (e.g. Ps 44) and of individual lament (e.g. Ps 56). Some of them go back to David, when he was fleeing from Absalom. Others reflect the period of exile (Ps 137). The movement within some Psalms, from early lament to resolution in trust and praise, is astounding (e.g. Ps 10.1–13 and

14–18; Ps 22.1–18 and 19–31 – the Psalm Jesus quoted on the cross). If you are being persecuted, delve into the depths of the Psalms.

A young Jewish girl was taken captive by the Arameans and became the servant of the wife of Naaman, the Syrian commander (2 Kings 5). When he was suffering from leprosy, she mentioned Elisha the prophet, who healed people in Israel. If you are a prisoner of war, God may use you for his purposes of healing and salvation.

The destruction of the Northern Kingdom by the Assyrians in the eighth century BC and the exile of the leading Jews in Babylon in the sixth century BC are presented in the Hebrew Scriptures (the prophets and Deuteronomic historians) as part of God's judgement on his wayward people.

The prophets in Babylon, especially the anonymous prophet whose words resound in the chapters 40–55 of the book of Isaiah, proclaimed that the Lord had not been defeated by the Babylonian gods, nor was he limited to the particular territory of Palestine, but was the God of the whole world. He is unique (there is only one God) because he is universal (he is the God of all heaven and earth). The Jews needed to be removed from their own land to understand the immensity of God. If you become a refugee in a strange land, you may glimpse new aspects of God.

The four 'Servant Songs' of the anonymous prophet in Babylon resound across the centuries: Isaiah 42.1–4; 49.1–6; 50.4–9; 52.13 – 53.12. The identity of the Servant seems to oscillate between the nation of Israel corporately (Isa 49.3) and the mysterious, yet quite definitely individual, person (Isa 49.5). The task of Israel becomes focused on him. 'He was despised and rejected by others; a man of suffering and acquainted with infirmity … He was oppressed, and he was afflicted, yet he did not open his mouth: like a lamb that is led to the slaughter, and like a sheep that before its shearers is silent, so he did not open his mouth' (Isa 53.3 and 7).

The Servant is reflected in the New Testament witness to Jesus. When you are under pressure, remember you are not alone, and you represent others who have gone before you. The Ultimate Other, Jesus the Servant of the Lord, in whom, and by whom, you are surrounded, has been through this suffering, pioneering the way.

The book of Esther resonates for people who are oppressed. Haman was the evil vizier at the court of the Persian King Ahasuerus (usually identified as Xerxes), who plotted the destruction of the Jews and is still seen as the archetypal persecutor. Through the wise and subtle interventions of Queen Esther, a Jew, they were delivered.

Mordecai, Esther's uncle, stirred her into action by expressing the key theological suggestion: 'Who knows? Perhaps you have come to royal dignity for just such a time as this' (Esth 4.14). At the festival of Purim, Jews still celebrate this particular deliverance and the defeat of Haman. If you have been raised up to an influential position, God can use you to protect the persecuted: be not silent.

Similarly, the book of Daniel brings comfort and strength to those under pressure. The book is bifocal. Set in the context of the exile in Babylon in the sixth century BC but probably written in the second century BC, it also reflects the horror inflicted on the Jews in Jerusalem by the Syrian despot Antiochus Epiphanes in the second century BC, and uses the exile narrative to encourage those facing these contemporary horrors. The Syrian king banned circumcision and the keeping of Jewish food laws and even sacrificed a pig on the temple altar. This is the archetypal 'desolating sacrilege' (KJV, 'the abomination of desolation') to which Jesus looked back in Matthew 24.15 and foresaw in the Roman destruction of the Temple, which happened within a generation in AD 70. Jesus drew his favourite title for himself, 'Son of Man', from Daniel 7.13–14 (KJV), which refers to those who are persecuted and vindicated: both a personal and a corporate figure.

Daniel, when threatened with the fiery furnace, stressed, 'If our God whom we serve is able to deliver us ... let him deliver us. But if not, be it known to you, O king, that we will not serve your gods and we will not worship the golden statue that you have set up' (Dan 3.17–18). If you are threatened, God may deliver you or he may not, but stand firm. When Daniel and his two friends were in the furnace, King Nebuchadnezzar was astounded, 'But I see four men unbound, walking in the middle of the fire, and they are not hurt; and the fourth has the appearance of a son of the gods' (Dan 3:25, KJV). God is with his people in the midst of their suffering.

In the Wisdom literature, the book of Job wrestles with God's inscrutable ways. The central poem portrays Job arguing with God and protesting his innocence in the face of his friends, who encouraged him to admit his sin. It seems to be a protest against another strand in the Wisdom tradition, shown especially in Proverbs, which taught that those who do wrong suffer and that those who do right are blessed.

The Apocrypha

In the Apocrypha, or Deutero-Canonical Books, which Anglicans read for 'example of life and instruction of manners' (Article VI), the persecution of the Jews by Antiochus Epiphanes is described in 1 Maccabees chapter 1, and in the next chapters the story of the Maccabean revolt, led by Judas Maccabees, is told.

Chapter 13 describes Judea gaining its independence. It is also in the books of Maccabees that the idea of martyrdom, and the development of the belief of life after death, is first presented to Jewish spirituality in a structured way.

The New Testament

Jesus of Nazareth grew up as a Jew under the oppressive colonial rule of Rome. He did not easily fit into any of the most prominent groups of Jews of his day, and had questions for all of them. The Sadducees were priests and members of powerful, wealthy, conservative old Jewish families. They denied the permanent validity of any laws except those in the Pentateuch, and rejected the later doctrines of resurrection, afterlife, angels, and demons. They reluctantly collaborated with the Romans and plotted to have Jesus killed. In discussing the doctrine of resurrection, Jesus deliberately quoted from the Pentateuch (Ex 3.6 in Mk 12.18–27) to show that

God was the God of the living: 'the God of Abraham, the God of Isaac, and the God of Jacob'.

The Pharisees were pious, holy, lay scholars, whose lives centred on the synagogue. However, their stress on the importance of keeping minute details of the oral law led to many seeing it as being burdensome. Jesus was strong in his condemnation of their hypocrisy. The Zealots followed the tradition of the Maccabean revolt and were part of a wider resistance movement. Living under Roman imperialism, they urged and practised guerrilla warfare and also struggled against Jewish collaborators. Jesus scandalized them by preaching love of enemies and non-violence. The Essenes, seeing themselves as 'sons of light' over against the 'sons of darkness', set up rigorous monasteries in the desert, turning their backs on the 'corrupt' Temple authorities, and copied out scriptural texts (e.g. the Dead Sea Scrolls of the Qumran community). Jesus may have been seen by them as a naive prophet who refused to follow their austerity. If you do not fit in with particular religious groupings, you may be a threat to them all.

Matthew, the scribe, gathers Jesus' radical teaching on mission and consequential suffering into chapter 10 of his gospel. 'See, I am sending you out like sheep into the midst of wolves; so be wise as serpents and innocent as doves' (10.16). Jesus continues with his extraordinary promise of the Spirit's inspiration: 'When they hand you over, do not worry about how you are to speak or what you are to say; for what you are to say will be given to you at that time; for it is not you who speak, but the Spirit of your Father speaking through you' (10.19–20). When you are persecuted, hear these key words across the centuries and the miles for your own witness in court.

Mark gathers Jesus' apocalyptic teaching into chapter 13 of his gospel. Jesus' prophecies of the end times were fulfilled in the Roman destruction of Jerusalem, within a generation, and will come to a climax at the end of ages. Christians live between these times. If you are under pressure for your faith, draw on the consolation of the coming Son of Man with his ultimate justice and judgement of God.

John dramatically portrays the enigmatic Jesus before the bewildered Pilate (chapters 18 and 19). The Ruler of all before the present ruler; the embodiment of Truth before the wondering governor; power face to face. "'Do you not know that I have power to release you, and power to crucify you?" Jesus answered him, "You would have no power over me unless it had been given to you from above'" (Jn 19.10–11). When you are brought before political leaders, remember the overarching power of God.

According to some manuscript traditions, on the cross, Jesus cried out, 'Father, forgive them; for they do not know what they are doing' (Lk 23.34). In context, this seems likely to refer to the Roman soldiers who were crucifying him. In 1 Corinthians 2.8, Paul wrote enigmatically, 'None of the rulers of this age understood this; for if they had, they would not have crucified the Lord of glory.' If you are suffering under alien regimes, remember you are joined together, for ever, with Christ the pioneer of forgiveness.

The resurrection of the Son of God, portrayed in the gospels and witnessed to in Acts, and into the 'wake' of which we are joined in faith and baptism (Rom 6), is foundational for any theology of surviving under persecution. If Jesus died and was raised to the glory of God the Father, then we, who are part of him, will also be raised. If you are under the most extreme pressure, remember this ultimate personal and corporate hope.

The early Church, in Acts, was persecuted and scattered, which led to wider horizons of witness. Luke portrays Peter as handing on the baton of witness and persecution to Paul. Peter and John stand up to the leaders of the Jews in the Sanhedrin, the Council, when they warn them not to speak of Jesus: 'Whether it is right in God's sight to listen to you rather than to God, you must judge; for we cannot keep from speaking about what we have seen and heard' (Acts 4.19–20).

Stephen, the first martyr, fulfilled Jesus' promise that the Holy Spirit would give words of witness: 'they could not withstand the wisdom and the Spirit with which he spoke' (Acts 6.10). After his powerful speech, applying the history of Israel to the coming of the Righteous One, and their fury, Stephen 'filled with the Holy Spirit … gazed into heaven and saw the glory of God and Jesus standing at the right hand of God' (Acts 7.55). Following his Master's pattern of forgiveness, his last prayer is 'Lord, do not hold this sin against them' (Acts 7.60). If you are called upon to bear witness to religious leaders for your faith, remember the strength, wisdom, and forgiveness of Peter, John, and Stephen, which are inspired by the Holy Spirit.

Saul approved of the stoning of Stephen. The persecutor then becomes the Apostle and is persecuted. Luke describes this dramatic turnaround three times (in Acts 9, and in Paul's words of witness to Jews in Jerusalem in chapter 22, and to King Agrippa in chapter 26). 'I asked, "Who are you, Lord?" The Lord answered, "I am Jesus whom you are persecuting. But get up and stand on your feet"' (Acts 26.15–16). When you are persecuted, Jesus is persecuted too.

Paul's lists his sufferings in 1 Corinthians chapter 4 and 2 Corinthians 11.23–33 and concludes, 'When reviled, we bless; when persecuted, we endure; when slandered, we speak kindly' (1 Cor 4.12–13). This echoes the sayings of Jesus. But he also stood on the ground of Roman justice, when he, as a Roman citizen, appealed to Rome (Acts 25). If you are treated unjustly according to the law, appeal.

Paul wrote four extraordinarily inspired letters from prison in Rome: Ephesians, Colossians, Philippians, and Philemon. If you are imprisoned for your faith, write: for God may give you insights in theology for the benefit of countless others after you. Write for yourself and for others.

The letter to the Hebrews was written to encourage Jewish Christians to hold firm to their faith. It draws on the human sufferings of Jesus (chapter 2) and the witness throughout the ages from Abel to the prophets (chapter 11) and bids them, 'Remember those who are in prison, as though you were in prison with them; those who are being tortured, as though you yourselves were being tortured' (Heb 13.3). If you are under pressure, you are not alone but are surrounded by a cloud of earlier witnesses. Christians throughout the world are remembering you as present with you.

The first letter of Peter may reflect the changed attitude of Roman authorities under the Emperor Domitian (AD 81–96): instead of tolerating Christians as a subset among the Jews, they were persecuted as being distinct and refusing to offer sacrifices to the 'divine' Emperor.

The book of Revelation has a subtle reference to the cult of the Emperor in Pergamum in 2.13: 'I know where you are living, where Satan's throne is. Yet you are holding fast to my name'. Revelation serves as a stimulus to stand firm under vicious pressure from the 'beast' of the Roman Empire. It is profound political theology for the persecuted. It is extraordinarily allusive, and reflective, of vast swathes of passages in the Old Testament. If such references were all hyperlinked, the whole book could well become blue in colour.

Its original message referred to the politics of its day in the Roman Empire, but persecution is perennial, and the book of Revelation is permanently warning and warming. God is in charge, is fighting to bring justice to his world, and this mysteriously includes the suffering of his people, as it did of his beloved Son.

If you are persecuted, remember the multitude from every tribe, tongue, people, and nation singing, 'Salvation belongs to our God who is seated on the throne, and to the Lamb! ... for the Lamb at the centre of the throne will be their shepherd, and he will guide them to springs of the water of life, and God will wipe away every tear from their eyes' (Rev 7.10 and 17).

Reflection and Response

A In the light of the overview of Scriptures, for each of the life studies i–vi and any other current examples of religious persecution:

1. Which biblical passages do you feel would be particularly helpful to consider?
2. How do you determine whether a biblical passage is appropriate or not for a particular current context?
3. Suggest examples of any biblical passages that it would be unhelpful to consider.
4. Are there other biblical passages, which have not been mentioned here, that you could helpfully apply to these life studies?

B Theological insights

1. What examples of seeing God's purposes, either within persecution or in bringing good out of suffering, can you see within the biblical passages?
2. Are any of these examples applicable to the life studies in Chapter 2, or to any other current examples of persecution?
3. In the light of your reflection upon Scripture and the different life studies and other current examples of religious persecution, what theological conclusions are you drawing about religious persecution?

C Response

1. Write a prayer of praise to thank God for the resources that we have within Scripture which we can apply to our daily lives and to the world.
2. Are there any things that you need to repent of, either personally or on behalf of your nation or church, with regard to either the misuse of Scripture or failure to act in the light of Scripture?
3. If possible, turn your theological conclusions from question B3 above into prayer.

4 Tradition

Introduction

Whatever point in lived history you choose to look at, there are human beings being persecuted. At our particular point in history, those of us who are Christians think especially of the Christians of the Middle and Near East, and we also think of victimized minorities who are not Christians. They have been forced to endure suffering, humiliation, degradation, and death; to flee hastily and to leave, in most cases for ever, their homes and churches which were in the heartlands of Christianity. Christianity is not alone, nor has it ever been alone, in being persecuted. Christianity itself has engaged, and still does engage, in persecution, internally and externally, on a variety of levels. In this way we are part of the problem while we aspire to being part of the solution. In the midst of both idealism and alarmism, we need to keep this perspective before us. Each persecution and each death by persecution is different and to be condemned utterly.

The backdrop of Christian life and witness is always that of Jesus Christ and the Scriptures. It is to the Scriptures that we go time and again to make sense of our experiences, whether joyful or tragic. They also help us to pattern our future and in this way to make some sense of past, present and future together. For those who enjoy a Northern Hemisphere lifestyle, such a pressing eschatology is well-nigh meaningless because it is not yet, or no longer, part of everyday experiences or expectations. But in other parts of the world it is the hope in the things which are not seen that matters and which gives meaning. Martyrdom and what we might call the theology 'from below' and all those whom this experience and this reflection stimulate and sustain need this type of hope. In the words of a contemporary

Anglican priest from the region of the Near and Middle East which in 2014 and 2015 has undergone wholescale human and historical destruction: 'Martyrdom is not seeking death for the sake of Christ; martyrdom is seeking life. But if asked to carry the cross to death, we need to be obedient.'[10]

This conversational comment draws together life and obedience in ways that are volcanic in their impact and also redemptive in their remit as martyrs inspire courage and humility; compassion for the other while suffering oneself; proclamation in the midst of annihilation. As in the death and resurrection of Jesus Christ, the impossibles are held together in the presence of God in martyrdom. From very early in the history of martyrdom, the day of the death of such a witnessing Christian was referred to as dies natalis, the day of new birth. Before the Edict of Milan (AD 313), martyrdom

10 See page 22.

equated with baptism; it was understood as a witness to Christ and as a celebration of incorporation into the Body of Christ of those who were faithful by courage and suffering. People would defer baptism until a time as close to their natural death as possible, avoiding besmirching baptism with sin.

The sharing of such 'birthdays of new life', or saints' days, across the expanding Christian Church created a 'calendar of experience'. Along with the 'calendar of the life of Christ and of the Holy Spirit', it formed the basis of the Liturgical Calendar, giving focus to fear and hope in times of recurring persecution. It is very important that the Christian Church today remember in this way the martyrs of our time in the crucible of Christianity and in other war-torn parts of the world. The development of cycles of prayer and the liturgical colour red link Evangelists and Martyrs. The active development of this solidarity on a regular, local basis across the Anglican Communion, together with the sharing of these martyr-days at a time when communication could hardly be easier, would of itself create and sustain a wave of connection. Martyrdom and the eschatological life of Jesus Christ combine as truly inspirational in the life of all Christians. They build and enliven Communion.

Early Period

The continuity of the biblical era into the era of the Early Church is one of growth through witness. Christianity initially was found in cities where Judaism was already established. Throughout the first three centuries, persecution was sporadic but intense when and where it happened. This is in no sense to diminish it or minimize it. The Church continued to offer the Christ-like service of its members to their neighbours and communities, irrespective of their faith or affiliation. Christianity and citizenship marched hand in hand as different but largely complementary loyalties. Citizenship gave Christian people an entitlement to presence. The theological starting point was the emerging clear distinction in the doctrine of God between Judaism and Christianity. The context of the Roman Empire was one of widespread toleration of local religions across a far-flung Empire.

The dissension between Judaism and Christianity showed that Christianity was not a national or a geographical religion but a diverging ideology and community based in faith and practice. In certain respects the Roman governmental system protected Christianity, refusing to accept anonymous evidence against Christians or to root them out in anti-Christian pogroms. The Romans were both religious and superstitious; they saw the safeguarding of the pax deorum (peaceful and therefore providential guidance of human affairs by the gods of both Rome and Greece) as pivotal to national and personal self-interest. This was what Christianity could be charged with threatening, as it had a missionary and expansionist world-view.

More sustained and systematic persecution was often triggered by other things happening in the Empire than by specific acts of violation by Christians. Christians became the obvious target after the destruction of the Jerusalem Temple (AD 70). The persecutions in the era of the Emperor Decius (AD 250) were the most sustained and located in the Roman province of North Africa. The common thread in the martyrologies is of apocalyptic interpretation of the experience of suffering and death; it is a thread running from the account of the martyrdom of Stephen (Acts 7) through to that of Janani Luwum in Uganda in 1977.[11] Under Decius it

11 See page 102.

had to do with public compliance with and enforced participation in the Roman religious cult for the well-being of the Emperor. The depths of this persecution stretched to the seizure of Scriptures and sacred vessels and under Diocletian in AD 303; it was further systematized to include imprisonment of Christian clergy and expulsion of Christians from army service and the imperial court.

The Edict of Toleration in AD 313 marked the recognition by Constantine the Great that there was a widespread need to offer toleration to all religions within a war-battered Empire. It was pivotal in a programme of reconstruction and in the building of integration for a vastly expanded Empire, recognizing that religion was important to the identity of disparate peoples and that Christianity was now to be included at the heart of the Imperial world. Christianity emerged as a force for good and for well-being for the Empire.

Those forces that created antagonism and flashpoints for persecution now ensured the stability of Christianity in a more tolerant society: diocesan and metropolitical structures ran hand in hand with the provision of civic government. This was subverted for eighteen months during the reign of Julian the Apostate (AD 361–3). He sought to establish Paganism as the religion of the Empire, following carefully, and replacing exactly, the ways in which Christianity had recently been institutionally established. In many ways this was the greatest compliment to Christianity although it set out to dismantle it.

The integration of Church and state is also seen in the seamless way in which Ambrose, a layman and provincial governor of Milan, was elected as bishop of Milan (AD 374). Another important consideration is the flourishing of the monastic movement in all its diversity in community and individual witness in the fourth and fifth centuries and, in a time of peace, the substitution of white (bloodless) martyrdom for red (violent) martyrdom. The interesting and terrifying thing is that many of these themes of persecution, martyrdom, and witness re-emerged regularly throughout the history of the Christian Church in its relations with the state and in the internal relationships within different branches of Christianity and between Christianity and other World Faiths. The eventual suppression of pagan cults by the Christian Roman Empire culminated in Theodosius' decree of AD 391.

Medieval Period

The Crusades

The term 'crusade' is highly emotive. Even to this day, in a highly secular context, it carries overtones of uncritical zeal in the cause of something powerful and dominant and of so much importance to the person concerned as to admit of no contradiction or opposition. Originating from a series of Western European Christian interventions, begun in 1095, in order to reclaim and retain the Holy Land from Islam and later to stem the advance of the Ottoman Empire, the word 'crusade' is derived from the Latin word for a cross. Crusaders were granted indulgences for services rendered to the Church, and they were accorded the status of martyr if they died in active service. The Crusades led to occasions of extreme brutality both to Jews at home and in Jerusalem and to the new subjects of the East, including Orthodox Christians and Muslims.

The Cathars, the Inquisition, and the Reformation

The Cathars or Albigensians claimed to be restoring the purity of the early Church. Starting around 1140 in Germany, their ideals and those of the emerging exponents of radical reform and the apostolic life showed significant similarities. Their theology showed marked signs of influence from parts of the Eastern Church in ways which were decidedly dualistic.[12] Their materialistic emphasis meant that they rejected sacraments, hell, purgatory, and the resurrection of the body, and also marriage and animal produce. Because this was too difficult a way of life for many people, further divisions developed between rigorists

12 Dualistic theology makes an accelerated distinction between the spiritual and the material.

and ordinary believers. The Church Catholic reacted by bringing to bear on the Cathars the reforms of the Fourth Lateran Council, the Dominican Order, and the Inquisition; Cathars were effectively obliterated by 1300.

The most notorious organ of orthodoxy undoubtedly was the Inquisition. Although the Fathers of the Church generally disapproved of physical penalties, the secular powers viewed heresy as treason, rewarding it with confiscation and death. In 1184 Pope Lucius III enabled bishops to make inquisition: holding special ecclesiastical tribunals for the detection of heresy in their dioceses, with the secular authorities punishing those who refused to recant. In 1233 Pope Gregory IX appointed full-time papal inquisitors from the Dominican and Franciscan Orders. The accused, interviewed in secret in the presence of sworn witnesses, were never told the charges against them nor allowed to call defence witnesses. Fearing the taint of abetting heresy, lawyers were reluctant to defend cases. Pope Innocent IV introduced torture in 1252, and the unrepentant were handed to the secular authorities and burnt alive.

The use and the range of Inquisition show its versatility and its cruelty as a tool of orthodoxy: for the repression of incipient sixteenth-century Italian Protestantism; of fifteenth-century nominally Christian Spanish Jews; and of sixteenth-century Muslims and Christians. The Inquisition also took complete control of the censorship of books. It was eventually wound up in Portugal in 1821 and in Spain in 1834.

English Reformation

The English Reformation can appear superficially to have been played out in the lives of royal celebrities, but the upheaval and cruelty experienced on the ground as religious priorities and ideologies were implemented as part of public policy in the lives of an overwhelmingly illiterate agrarian population are incalculable. A traditionalist in doctrine and church government, Henry VIII brought about the overthrow of Papal Supremacy and the Dissolution of the Monasteries, largely in pursuit of short-term political and personal ends. Under Edward VI the influence of Continental Reformers, including Peter Martyr, Bucer, and Zwingli, is much clearer, with significant changes and impositions regarding ritual and practice: a Book of (prescribed) Homilies, a Book of Injunctions including the condemnation of pictures and all lights in churches except the two before the Blessed Sacrament. The Act of Uniformity (1549) imposed by penal legislation the use of the First Book of Common Prayer, followed by the more Protestant Second Book of Common Prayer (1552). This was a seismic re-definition of the Church of God in the minds of the people accustomed to the comfort and the continuum of the Middle Ages. With persecution for non-compliance, changes included the destruction of altars, which were replaced by wooden tables, the attack on the doctrine of Real Presence, and the giving of Communion in both kinds. Thomas Wyatt's plot against Mary Tudor (1554) made her Catholic rule more severe. As Jane Grey and the future Queen Elizabeth were sent to the Tower of London, the heresy laws were restored and trials for heresy began (1554). Persecution and the burning of Cranmer, Latimer, Ridley, and Hooper, and Mary's general unpopularity, fuelled the Protestant cause. Elizabeth I dismantled unpopular aspects of Mary's regime. She combined Protestant content, particularly preaching, with sufficient Catholic components to create a Settlement veering in a Protestant direction. Elizabeth waged war against five countries: Scotland, France, the Netherlands, Spain, and Ireland. The defeat of the

Spanish Armada in 1588 was presented as evidence that God had chosen her to rule. This came at the height of her persecution of Roman Catholics, which had begun in 1583. Elizabeth's persecution of Roman Catholics was in response to the plotting against her that followed on from her excommunication in 1570 by Pope Pius V, who formally released her subjects from allegiance to her, and an upsurge of popular Protestantism making conservative concessions less necessary. Such persecution was vigorously pursued from 1585 to 1591, including the execution of Mary, Queen of Scots, like other Roman Catholics, on a charge of treason.

The Reformation in England and Ireland brought martyrdom and persecution of both Catholics and Protestants. After much bloodshed and cruelty there emerged a creative, peaceful, but uneasy compromise with tensions always remaining close to the surface. While being in one sense a forceful reminder that 'the blood of the martyrs is the seed of the church' (Tertullian) and with both the Anglican and Roman Catholic traditions alive in England and Ireland to this day, it is also a reminder that compromise comes all too often as a result of horrific killing in the name of religion.

The Modern Era: Genocide and Persecution

The later history of persecution has shown Christianity to be capable of initiating internal persecution of fellow Christians as well as giving and receiving persecution from those of other World Faiths.

Genocide

The term 'genocide' refers to the crime of intending to destroy, in whole or in part, a national, ethnical, racial, or religious group. Genocide is usually an instrument of the state. In the modern era the term is first used with regard to the Armenian Genocide, which involved the systematic destruction of one ethnic and religious grouping, Armenian Christians, by another, Turkish Muslims, from 1915 until 1923. Over two thousand Armenian communities across the Ottoman Empire were destroyed within months, and eventually more than one and a half million people were killed.

This genocide engendered flight from home, and the individual accounts of flight by the families of survivors take us to locations once again familiar today as arenas of conflict and war, such as Basra in Iraq. Armenians settled as far away as Harbin, China, and to this day remain an international diaspora. Many Armenians find deep resonances with their own ethnic experiences in the contemporary events of beheading, rape, and starvation of Christians and others in the Middle and Near East. The Armenian Genocide is immortalized in the words of Adolf Hitler, as he transferred the principle and the practice to the systematic annihilation of another ethnic and religious grouping, the Jews: 'Who today remembers the Armenians?'

The Shoah, the systematic massacre of the Jews under the Nazi regime (also known as the Holocaust), is the iconic genocide of the twentieth century. People of faith and humanity unite around this violation of humanity itself and the wanton destruction of the human person as an entity with dignity, independence, and honour. Religious identity and historic ethnicity were systematically eroded with the ideological intention of extinction through degradation, mockery, and annihilation. Other groups of people, including Roma and homosexual persons, were deliberately extirpated from the face of humanity with an unquestioned sense of entitlement to cleanse. The conflation of politics and science, of rhetoric and extermination, leaves the world in a state of numbness many decades later as we continue to wonder how people could pass by and let the murder of more than six million Jewish people and two and a half million Roma happen – simply for the fact that they were alive. The world has not recovered from this wilful degradation and extermination of near-manic proportions, nor can it readily do so. We remember with deepest sadness as well as the ethnic massacres in Rwanda (1994) and Bosnia-Herzegovina (1992–5).

Communist Persecution

The example of Russia draws us right back to the persecutions of the first Christians. While Marxism challenged everything bourgeois, including bourgeois Christianity, holding that spirituality is a transcendent egotism and an unwillingness to share the sufferings of the world and humanity, Berdyaev (1874–1948), speaking from within this intellectual persecution, said: 'Bread for myself is a material question; bread for my neighbour is a spiritual question.' Lenin turned totalitarian theory into political reality across Europe, leading to governments which made absolute claims not only over the structures of society but over truth itself in challenging and intimidating scientists, artists, intellectuals, and religious bodies. Lenin was ambiguous about persecution, knowing that religion thrives on it. Dialectical materialism appeals emotionally to but a few; many of what were called the Warsaw Pact countries became Communist by finding themselves in the wrong place after the Second World War rather than by any elective democratic vote or decision. The principles and ethics by which the Church stands are radically different in their motivation from those of Communism.

Before the Bolshevik Revolution of 1917, Russia as an Orthodox country had persecuted and expelled Jesuits; and problems had been caused in Poland and Lithuania by Roman Catholic espousal of the nationalist cause. The reorganization of ecclesiastical life in Russia in 1917–18 was disrupted by the Revolution. The progressives and the conservatives in the Church were persecuted indiscriminately: the Church was deprived of its right to own property. During the famine of 1921–2 the state took all church valuables. Any resistance was used as a pretext to arrest clergy, and large numbers were condemned to death or banished to prison camps. Lenin decreed that formal teaching of religion to anyone aged under 18 years was a criminal offence; monasteries and theological schools were closed. Muslims, Jews, and Buddhists were equally persecuted, and the Roman Catholic Church in Russia virtually ceased to exist.

In 1929 Stalin introduced a law on religious associations which prepared the way for the suppression of religion during the Great Purge of 1934–7. The Constitution of 1936 proclaimed freedom of religious worship as well as granting the organs of state freedom to disseminate anti-religious propaganda. By 1939 only a few hundred churches remained open, with very few clergy. Metropolitan Sergius's support for the war effort, after the German invasion in 1941, resulted in the opening of churches, seminaries, academies, and some monasteries, and Sergius was made Patriarch. However, the defeat of Germany and the increasing tension between the USSR and the West resulted in the resurgence of anti-religious propaganda. Persecution in Russia of Christians, not only the Orthodox, continued until the Glasnost of President Gorbachev, when concessions and new legislation were promised in return for the Church's help in rebuilding society. A similar but locally nuanced and diverse story can be told, with subtle differences, of the Baltic States, predominantly Lutheran, and Ukraine, predominantly Uniate, that is Orthodox in practice and Roman in obedience.

Albania is a special case in Europe in that it was the first country in the world officially to be declared atheist. The systematic persecution of Christianity followed, and Islam survived on the technicality of being a cultural entity. The restoration of religious freedom in 1990 has resulted in the re-flourishing of Orthodoxy and Roman Catholicism and also the active presence of Protestantism in Albania.

Dietrich Bonhoeffer

Bonhoeffer (1906–45) was a Lutheran pastor who in 1930s Germany opposed the Nazi movement from the outset. He was pivotal in the Confessing Church, becoming head of its Finkenwald Seminary in 1935. He was opposed to the German Christians who tried to synthesize Nazism and Christianity. Some of these wished to eliminate the Old Testament, St Paul the Rabbi, and St Augustine's teaching with what they considered as his 'Jewish' idea of sin; the Holy Land was not in Palestine but in Germany, and Hitler was the embodiment of the law of God. The professed aim of the German Christians who supported Hitler was to 'complete' Martin Luther's Reformation. They had the leadership of more than half of the national church during the Second World War.

For Bonhoeffer, martyrdom was set in this escalating and idolatrous context, which he opposed theologically and ecclesiologically. He put his intellect at the service of opposition. While Bonhoeffer may be most remembered for his religion-less Christianity, other aspects of theology are important in understanding his personal martyrdom. His sermon rejecting the Führer Principle and embracing the Cross was a direct confrontation with German Christians and outlines one aspect of Bonhoeffer's theology of martyrdom:

God's victory means our defeat, means our humiliation; it means God's mocking anger at all human arrogance, being puffed up, trying to be important in our own right. It means reducing the world and its clamour to silence; it means the crossing through of all our ideas and plans, it means the Cross.[13]

Bonhoeffer is very clear about the link between Christology and ecclesiology, and the solidarity with Christ on the part of the church member. This comes through in his 1933 Lectures on Christology: 'The concept of the body, applied to the Church, is not merely a functional concept, relevant only to the members of this body; but in its comprehensiveness and centrality it is a concept of him who is present, exalted and humbled.' This is complemented by the challenge he offers in the definition of truth in the same series: truth is not something which rests in itself

13 From Bonhoeffer's 1933 Lectures on Christology.

and for itself, but something which takes place between two persons. Truth happens in community. It is these strands of theology which contribute significantly to the martyrdom of Bonhoeffer and shows us the connection with a wider world and understanding of the Church as a Christ-like community.

Uganda and Luwum

Occasions of martyrdom in Africa abounded throughout the nineteenth and twentieth centuries. Significant among these for Anglicans is the martyrdom of Archbishop Janani Luwum, killed on the orders of Idi Amin in February 1977.[14] Luwum is synonymous with resistance to the regime of Idi Amin and is remembered for his Christ-like graciousness.[15]

14 Luwum's image is sculpted on the western façade of Westminster Abbey among the 'martyrs of the twentieth century'; the statues also include Oscar Romero, the Roman Catholic Archbishop of El Salvador, assassinated by a state death squad in March 1980.

15 The book *Uganda Holocaust: They Faced Amin's Terror Machine*

The Christ-like language used by Luwum in prison is poignant: 'You are hitting me, but I am innocent and I have done nothing. You are hitting me because you have power, but you would not have this power if it had not been given you by God.' And his oppressor is cast in the role of Pontius Pilate.

The gathering of the faithful at the empty grave of Luwum at Namirembe Cathedral in Kampala is striking: 'Instead of being something that discourages us, the empty grave spoke to us of the victory that we have over death; that whatever happens to a person's body, there is an everlasting life that is quite indestructible.'[16] The grave was empty because Luwum's body was never handed back to the family or the church for burial. The

---

Undaunted by Dan Wooding and Ray Barnett (Grand Rapids, MI: Zondervan, 1980) draws this out in significant ways, taking us into the centrality of imitation of Christ in the witness which is martyrdom.'

16 Ibid., p. 103.

further resonance with the early years of the Roman Empire is in the recorded fact that while a month-long vigil was kept at the grave of Luwum, Idi Amin was declared Emperor and Son of God.

This martyrdom of Christians in Uganda was not the first. In 1885 three young servant boys were condemned to death in an effort to stamp out Christianity. The apocalyptic resonance with the book of Daniel is clear in the message the boys sent to the king at their execution: 'tell His Majesty that he has put our bodies in the fire, but we won't be in the fire for long. Soon we will be with Jesus, which is much better. But ask him to repent and change his mind, or he will land in a place of eternal fire and desolation.' Part of the reason for their execution was their refusal, in the understanding of the Ugandan Anglican tradition, to accede to King Mwanga's homosexual requests of them.

Daesh

In the twenty-first century we have found ourselves facing the sustained extirpation of Christianity in the Middle East and the Near East together with other groups of people such as women and elderly and homosexual people. These people have for long been hoping for the benefits of a freedom, and particularly since the Arab Spring, which derives from the best expression of Western liberal thought and for the holding up of the mirror of human rights to the worst excesses of societal repression. The comprehensive dismantling of memory and history and culture by Daesh and by those who are allied to it links with a currently uncontrolled and uncontrollable sense of entitlement to kill those who represent, in whatever way and for whatever reason, a life lived outside this particular distorted cocktail of Islamic ideas.

Every generation seems to promise the next generation that it will never happen again. It continues to happen again, and the major differences seem to be the sophistication and the escalation of the cruelty along with the depth of the iconoclasm. All of this is combined with a globalized communications network, with the trafficking of women and girls, and with oil. It is combined also with the recruitment of radicalized youth, male and female, from the various international diasporas which have themselves been caused by warfare, terrorism, and enforced emigration. It is in no sense primitive but it is brutal, inhumane, and dehumanizing. It is throwing up contemporary martyrs on a daily basis. If we go to YouTube or any search engine we can call up plenty of well-documented martyrologies which can take their place as contemporary history alongside inherited annals of the martyrs.

Postscript

Following the release of the Daesh video depicting the beheading of twenty-one Coptic Christian workers in Libya, the Bible Society of Egypt produced a publication containing the following short poem in colloquial Arabic which draws attention to the dilemma at the heart of terrorism and victimhood:

- Who fears the other?
- The row in orange, watching paradise open?
- Or the row in black, with minds evil and broken?

The colour-coding is significant. The black derives from Daesh; the orange derives ultimately from rendition and Guantanamo Bay.

These events are depicted in the icon on the front cover of this publication.

The dilemma of martyrdom continues, worked out for all of the world to see in an age of digital globalization and of global digitization, with all of the question marks around modernity, whatever the era.

Reflection and Response

A In the light of the overview of Tradition, for each of the life studies i–vi and any other currents examples of persecution:

1. Do any of these historical examples have helpful parallels?
2. Are any historical examples unhelpful if we try to apply them to these life studies?

B For each of the following quotations, consider how they may apply for those within the life studies, and also for yourself as part of the Body of Christ:

1. 'Martyrdom is not seeking death for the sake of Christ; martyrdom is seeking life. But if

asked to carry the cross to death, we need to be obedient' (quoted on p 22 and p 77).

2. 'The blood of the martyrs is the seed of the church' (Tertullian – quoted on page 92 and implied in the reference to Lenin on page 96).
3. 'God's victory means our defeat, means our humiliation; it means God's mocking anger at all human arrogance, being puffed up, trying to be important in our own right. It means reducing the world and its clamour to silence; it means the crossing through of all of our ideas and plans, it means the Cross' (Bonhoeffer – quoted on page 101).
4. 'But you would not have this power if it had not been given you by God' (Luwum – quoted on page 103).
5. 'Who fears the other? The row in orange, watching paradise open? Or the row in black,

with minds evil and broken?' (Bible Society of Egypt – quoted on page 107).

C Response

1. Write a prayer of praise to celebrate God's faithfulness.
2. In the light of the material in this chapter, are there any issues or attitudes that you wish to repent of, either for yourself or on behalf of your nation or church?
3. In the light of your reflection upon Tradition and the different life studies and other current examples of religious persecution, are you drawing any additional theological conclusions about religious persecution which can be turned into prayer?
4. Consider whether material used here could enrich your regular prayer life.

5 Reason

Anglicans look to the primacy of Scripture, interpreted with the aid of Tradition and Reason, to guide them. Chapters 3 and 4 have explored the first two dimensions; in this chapter we look at various aspects of the third.

The *Virginia Report* of 1997 explains: 'If tradition is the mind that Christians share as believers and members of the Church, reason is the mind they share as participants in a particular culture' (paras 3.8–3.11, at para 3.9). In this chapter, we first explore the contributions to 'reason', in the sense of the mind of contemporary believers, made by four great currents of cultural influence which have shaped powerful theological approaches, respectively from feminists, from black Christians, and from those committed to two different movements of liberation. While these are all reflective of ways in which secular thinking can inform our understanding of the Gospel, other religious faiths also exert a strong influence on particular cultures, and so in looking at the role of 'reason' in this chapter, we will also need to take account of these too.

Theological Responses

Four recent theologies are worth commenting upon.

i Feminist Theology

Feminist Theology asks hermeneutical questions from the standpoint of justice issues. The inherited male focus of the Bible is challenged to see the experience of women as a starting point and a norm. Reformist (or Liberation) Feminist Theology articulates human liberation as the central message of the Bible and seeks to work, in this way, within the Christian tradition. The hermeneutics of suspicion are an invitation to have women re-enter the centre stage of biblical response and witness as in early Christianity. The mechanism of critical engagement with the inherited biblical tradition (and not all models of Feminist Theology wish to do this) is through a renewed understanding of covenant. In this model, based on Genesis 1.27, the calling is common to women and to men; it is to serve God in mutual obligation to God and one another and in unity with one another and the creation. This has to combine with the hermeneutic of eschatology, which challenges prevailing cultures and points to Christ as the transformer and the one who challenges and re-focuses our current social settings. The most potent of these is the articulation of the era of the Spirit in Acts 2, where daughters and sons, female and male slaves prophesy.

The hermeneutical lens of Womanist Theology uses the experience of African American women and women of colour to reflect on theological tradition and interpretation of Scripture in seeking liberation. First named by Alice Walker in her book, *In Search of our Mother's Gardens: Womanist Prose* (1983), this work has been developed and deepened by the theologians Jacquelyn Grant, Delores Williams, and Katie Cannon. With roots in Black Theology, Womanist Theology expands this theological perspective as well as those of Feminist Theology and Liberation Theology. A Womanist theological perspective understands Jesus as a 'divine co-sufferer'[17] and seeks to ensure that the cultural context of oppressed people is the starting point for theological practice and action. Womanist

17 Jacquelyn Grant, 'Womanist Theology: Black Women's Experience as a Source for Doing Theology, with Special Reference to Christology', in James H. Cone and Gayraud S. Wilmore (eds.), *Black Theology: A Documentary History, 1980–1992* (Maryknoll, NY: Orbis Books, 1993), 281; see also Grant's fuller treatment *White Women's Christ and Black Women's Jesus: Feminist Christology and Womanist Response*. Brown Studies in Religion, 84 (Atlanta, GA: Scholars Press, 1989).

theologies would find common cause with many developing theologies around the globe.

ii Black Theology

Black Theology, a response of black church leaders to the Civil Rights Movement in the USA in the 1960s, similarly challenges institutions of exclusion. Its raison d'être is the correlation of the experience of exclusion and oppression on the grounds of race rather than gender and the confident overlapping of black identity and the Gospel of Jesus Christ. It therefore represents the elevation of ethnicity and colour into a theological category of inescapably positive proportions.

The fulcrum of the argument is that black people did not reject the Gospel brought to them by white oppressors but found in it a truth authenticated by suffering, and developed from it an indigenous religion orientated to freedom and human welfare. The liberation offered in a black Jesus is iconic of the freedom denied to black people in the white Christianity. At its most radical, therefore, Black Theology states that the salvation of white people can come about only by entering into this black consciousness of Jesus Christ even if it is not their direct personal experience. Ethnicity and liberation fulfil the role in Black Theology that gender and liberation do in Feminist Theology.

The South African Black Theology, unlike the broad sweep of American Black Theology, puts the love of God rather than revolution at the heart of God's liberating acts for God's people. This means that black power is the resumption by black people of their responsibility as whole human beings. The power therefore lies in the being itself, and it is the reclaiming of being black as being human which is the motive force. What is important here is that South African Black Theology also stands within African Christian theology, which emphasizes the role of the African pre-Christian religious heritage as a *praeparatio evangelica* (preparedness for the Gospel) and therefore enabling Christianity, despite its many residual features of missionary colonialism, to give voice to African cultural sensitivities. Its expression depends on the prevailing trends in any particular church and country. The movement in general is dependent on the primary addressing of identity as a key issue in theological reflection and self-understanding. And martyrdom forces issues of identity.

iii Liberation Theology

Liberation Theology is a third resource which has emerged in relation to exclusion from social and theological discourse in the twentieth century. As with both Feminist and Black Theology there is the need always to recognize that there is more than one theology and there are in fact different theologies of interpretation. The interpretative key is that Liberation Theology sets itself the task of interpreting the Christian faith from the perspective of the poor and the oppressed. This speaks directly into the situation of the persecuted in a local and tangible way. There is solidarity beyond analysis and there is solidarity before analysis. The question being asked is: 'Where is the God of justice in a world of injustice?' The human face of this theology is the derivation of theology from the victim, from a commitment to the poor and to non-persons.

Liberation Theology invites all of those who think and pray theologically to tunnel down and to make radical decisions for justice beyond the confusion, to which we are all susceptible, of the righteousness of God with human self-righteousness. As one of its founding fathers, Gustavo Gutiérrez, says: 'The poor deserve preference not because they are morally or religiously better than others, but because God is God, in whose eyes "the last are first." This statement clashes with our narrow understanding of justice; this very preference reminds us, therefore, that God's ways are not our ways.'[18] It is but an outworking of Matthew 5.44–45 in economic rather than meteorological circumstances. Liberation Theology shares Moltmann's theology of hope and Bonhoeffer's theology of religion in a secular space together with the rejection of any dualism between the Church and the world. However, the seismic shift in theological understanding of Vatican II is the deepest inspiration of Liberation Theology. Pope Francis is clearly aware of this context and speaks from within it and to it as he speaks to the city and the world. The point at which Liberation Theology gives theological voice to the poor is in and from the Base Ecclesial Communities. Such

18 Gustavo Gutiérrez, A Theology of Liberation: History, Politics, and Salvation, trans. and ed. Sister Caridad Inda and John Eagleson (1988), www.scribd.com/doc/206546534/A-Theology-of-Liberation-Gutierrez, p. 36 (accessed 16 May 2016).

communities are grass-roots communities of the lay poor who meet to pray, study the Bible, and wrestle with social and political issues contextually.

The theological relevance of Liberation Theology to the persecuted is significant and sustained, although this trajectory needs to be worked out in each new context with appropriate relevance rather than being downloaded uncritically. First it argues that theology must start from below; the poor and excluded are not seen as objects of Gospel pity but as those who shape and craft a new humanity in Christ. Secondly it argues for the integrity of context and the 'now' of eschatology. Thirdly it argues for praxis to the effect that theology is to be done rather than simply learned. The challenge to the Anglican Communion is the challenge in this regard of Liberation Theology: theology itself follows praxis.

iv Dalit Theology

Dalit Theology is a specific expression of a Theology of Liberation. It addresses head on the exclusion from the social system and from membership of society itself a group of people who are 'outside the caste system'. It gives freedom and dignity to human beings by means of a Christian theology of the human person as made in the image and likeness of God. Through this, the Dalits are an inspiration to others who suffer not only persecution but annihilation and classification as non-persons living outside the reality of this world.

For those who today suffer as members of minorities and are deprived of primary identity their experience is that of praxis and powerlessness. Liberation Theology is not for everyone, nor is it without proper criticism. It has the weakness of accepting and progressing the agenda of praxis as structured around the ultimately Marxist pre-understanding of social clash as a given beyond criticism. At its most reductionist, it is ultimately no more than any other form of human autonomy in the face of divine revelation of the self of God. However impossibly painful it may seem, God is the God of primary creation, not of secondary analysis or accommodation or indeed revolution. However difficult it becomes, Liberation Theology draws us into the recognition that context, particularly when it is squalid and destructive, is the primary experience of more and more people of the creation that God declared good.

Participating in a World Shaped by Many Faiths and Beliefs

The great Anglican missiologist Max Warren is credited with remarking that 'It takes a whole world to know the whole Gospel.' Our whole world is shaped by many different faiths and beliefs, and therefore in order to see how reason unfolds the meaning of the

Gospel for Anglican Christians today it is helpful to look at the attitudes to persecution held within other religious traditions. Indeed, Anglicans have used their scholarship in many ways over the centuries to explore and to understand religions other than their own. Particularly from the great missionary movement of the nineteenth century onwards, Anglican writers and researchers were among those most committed to the development of what was originally known as 'comparative religion', and they remain today extensively involved in the phenomenological, sociological, and theological study of religion. As much of this scholarship took its origin from times of religious conflict and intense religious change, it is not surprising that issues of persecution and religious violence have always fallen within its scope.

In what follows, we shall briefly describe attitudes to religious persecution in six great world traditions –

Judaism, Islam, Hinduism, Sikhism, Buddhism, and secularism – in order to understand better the context within which the Church witnesses today. Of course, these do not represent the totality of the world's faiths, and it is important to remember that some of the smaller religious traditions have experienced severe degrees of persecution – for example, the Yazidis, the Baha'is, or the Sikhs (who are mentioned briefly here). Nor can the range of teaching and attitudes they embrace be adequately summarized within the space we have; but even this cursory survey will show the way in which these issues reveal deeply held attitudes within the religious world. Given the context of our times, particularly in the Western world, it also seems right to supplement these with some mention of secularist thinking, as this plays a major philosophical role in shaping much which passes for 'reason' in the West today.

i Judaism

Throughout the Christian era, the threat or reality of persecution has been a shaping factor in Jewish life, and specifically Christian pressures have made a major contribution to this. Antisemitism was common in the classical world, but the triumph of Christianity added a theologically based anti-Judaism finding expression in a 'teaching of contempt' for Jewish religion and Jewish people. While official Church teaching insisted on the need to preserve the Jewish community, albeit in a position of humiliation, it also sanctioned aggressive proselytism, and at times forced conversions. Meanwhile, the Church's teaching, preaching, and liturgy fed a popular suspicion of and hostility towards Jewish people which frequently erupted into violence and murder. This toxic atmosphere provided the background to the rise of modern antisemitism, culminating in the unspeakable tragedy of the Shoah. In the last fifty years, the Christian churches have made a decisive effort to turn away from teachings and practices which both sanction anti-Judaism and encourage antisemitism, and to reappraise their theology in light of the Shoah.

Jewish communities in the diaspora developed deep and powerful theologies of exile and persecution. Among the themes present in these are: the belief that suffering can be a paradoxical sign of divine favour, as the Lord disciplines the child whom he loves; the mystical conviction that the divine glory, *shekinah*, has accompanied the people of Israel into exile, remaining with them as long as they study the Torah; the recognition of martyrdom, in the sense of refusal even to death to abandon Jewish practice and belief, as a way in which the name of God is glorified; and the strong, persistent longing of dispersed Jewish communities to be returned by God to the Holy Land, coupled with the expectation of the eventual re-establishment, in God's time, of the Temple in Jerusalem. In reaction on the one hand to movements encouraging assimilation into Western societies which nevertheless remained obdurately antisemitic, and on the other hand to a pious passivity which was content to wait for divine intervention to remedy Israel's dispersion and suffering, from the nineteenth century onwards, the Zionist movement actively promoted through human agency the return to Palestine of Jewish people, holding up a new ideal of the Jew as active pioneer and creator of his or her own destiny.

In the twentieth century, the incalculable horror of the Shoah, immediately followed by the triumph of Zionism in establishing the State of Israel, has produced a new set of configurations in Jewish attitudes to persecution and to martyrdom. While old themes, reflecting on suffering as in some sense a way of understanding the divine purpose, persist in communities both in Israel and in the diaspora, the new reality of a Jewish state, shaped from terrible trauma and always experiencing existential threat in the current Middle East, has led to a robustly activist stance of self-defence among many Jews, both secular and religious.

In this new context, there is a huge range of attitudes to the place of persecution in Jewish life, and this range is both linked to and complicated by an equally wide spectrum of views on the current political realities of the State of Israel in its Middle Eastern context. There remains much in traditional Jewish attitudes which can enrich and deepen Christian understanding of persecution and martyrdom, and much in contemporary attitudes which can sharply challenge us; our learning can be particularly sharpened when we are exposed to Jewish interpretations of those parts of the Scriptures which we share.

ii Islam

The first Muslims who gathered around Muhammad in Mecca experienced persecution of varying degrees at the hands of their pagan neighbours. In response to this, there developed the twin principles of *hijra*, migration to seek protection in a secure environment, and *jihād*. The Arabic word *jihād* means, in general, 'struggle', and can be used by individual Muslims to refer in the first place to the inner moral struggle within the soul. In a political sense, though, *jihād* means a struggle to establish the supremacy of Islam. According to tradition, one of the first places of asylum sought by the Islamic community was the Christian kingdom of Abyssinia. At the same time, the Qur'ān lauded those who died in the cause of God as 'witnesses' or 'martyrs' (*shuhada*). The concept may have roots in the Christian cult of the martyrs, but in Islam it unambiguously includes those responsible for the deaths of others, provided that they are fighting with steadfastness and courage in the cause of God. It must be stressed, though, that Islamic scholarship has consistently denied the title of 'martyr' to those who deliberately kill themselves, and that it has also insisted on the limitation of war to exclude the targeting of non-combatants.

Through much of Islamic history, the majority of Sunni Muslims have lived in societies which purport to be governed according to Islamic norms. In these situations, claims of persecution have typically centred on the assertion that so-called Islamic governments are really no such thing, and that the practice of authentic Islam invites harassment, exclusion, imprisonment, or death. At other times, Muslims have experienced ethnic cleansing, mass murder, or even genocide at the hands of communities of other faiths: for Christians, incidents such as the capture of Jerusalem during the First Crusade or the massacre at Srebrenica in the Bosnian War are a particular cause for shame and repentance. In the post-Muslim context of Spain after the Catholic 'reconquest', those who secretly clung to their Islamic identity were subject to inquisition, and to dire penalties if exposed.

If Sunni Islam cannot be said to have an advanced 'theology of persecution', as distinct from an episodic history of conflict, dispossession, and marginalization, the situation is different in Shi'a Islam, looking as it does for its formative history not only to the event of the Qur'ān but also to the disastrous battle of Karbala and the tragic death of Hussain. This seminal experience of persecution and martyrdom, constantly remembered in the present through passion plays focusing on Karbala, has become central to the spirituality of most Shi'a Muslims, and for many it has been accompanied by the experience of living as a minority in a more or less hostile environment. Together with a depth of reflection on the place of suffering in the life of faith, and a commitment to emulate the heroic integrity of Hussain, this has led to an emphasis of the idea of *taqiya*, an appropriate reserve or dissimulation to preserve the continuity of the faithful community under conditions of persecution.

In the contemporary world, conflicts between Shi'a and Sunni seem as pronounced as at any time in history, as do divisions among Sunni Muslims. At the same time, as a result of modern communications, many Muslims are being made painfully aware of experiences of suffering or victimhood on the part of their co-religionists in other parts of the world. To what extent a sense of grievance may give birth to a theology of persecution, and who can be accounted as a genuine martyr of Islam, are live issues today.

iii Hinduism

The designation 'Hinduism' is misleading if taken to indicate an identifiable religion with unified beliefs and practices of organization; Hindu societies have been notably pluriform in their religious, cultural, and social lives. There is a sense in which Hinduism became defined at all only in response to the threats either of outside incursions (particularly Islamic and Christian) or of internal dissensions (in such movements as Buddhism and Jainism). Within the complex Hindu world, religious discourse has been used to justify, and also at times to criticize, the internal stratification of classes or castes – a system which has sometimes degenerated into experiences of oppression, exclusion, or discrimination which in religious terms could be described as persecution. While some Dalits have turned to Islam, Christianity, Buddhism, or secular ways of thinking as sources of resistance and liberation, others have found identity and confidence in their own Hindu traditions of belief and practice.

Classical Hindu attitudes to violence and injustice commend two kinds of response. One is that of *ahimsa*, the force of non-violent resistance. This is by no means a passive quiescence; as exemplified by Gandhi, it has proved to be a powerful motor for transformation and reconciliation, while Gandhi's own death also shows how this costly path can generate its own martyrs – in this case, ironically, in being killed by a Hindu nationalist. The other response to injustice recognized in Hinduism is that of righteous warfare, and in some readings of Indian history this comes to be identified with the struggle against invasion or colonization from outside, whether Islamic or European. This struggle too has its heroes and martyrs, such as the Marathi warrior Shivaji and his son Sambhaji, gruesomely executed by the Mughal regime. Narratives of persecution in this history speak of attacks on Hindu religion and culture both physical, in the destruction of temples and the murder of devotees, and emotional, in attempts to win converts to another faith.

It is from appeal to a background such as this, compounded by the mass bloodshed experienced (on both sides) at the time of the Partition of India in 1947, that *Hindutva*, the resurgent movement of Hindu nationalism, derives its emotional force. Theologically, a sharp contrast is drawn between, on the one hand, a relaxed Hindu pluralism which is easily able to accommodate a variety of religions, and, on the other hand, the exclusivism and fanaticism which are alleged to be inextricable from monotheism. Politically, perceptions of victimhood are kept alive by the experience of Hindu minorities in and refugees from Pakistan, and to some extent Bangladesh. Nevertheless, in Western countries Hindu communities sometimes complain of being unwittingly caught up in hostility against Muslims.

iv Sikhism

Deriving from the Hindu society of Punjab, but with a faith and spirituality which are quite distinctive, Sikhism presents a striking instance of the development of a theology of persecution and of martyrdom. A devotional community gathered around a charismatic preacher of monotheism found it necessary, in response to attacks from oppressive Mughal rulers, to commit itself to armed resistance in defence of freedom and justice. Two of the then gurus who led the community are revered as martyrs, with the sacrifice of their lives being offered for Hindus as well as Sikhs. The spirit of militant resistance has remained a key component of Sikh theology ever since.

v Buddhism

The Buddhist scriptures in several places praise the virtues of forbearance and patience under suffering inflicted by others, and these can be said to be central Buddhist attitudes to persecution. Buddhism has generally sought to inculcate an ethic of non-violence, equanimity, and compassion, applying this with particular immediacy to members of the monastic community, but also holding it up as an ideal to lay followers. Following this path of non-violence, Buddhist monks in some situations have actively borne a martyr's witness to peace and justice. In some cases, this has even extended to the practice of self-immolation as a dramatic way of drawing attention to perceived injustice; perhaps the most celebrated instance of this, the death of the monk Thich Quang Du, was in fact a protest against policies of the then Vietnamese government, which were seen as unfairly privileging Christianity over Buddhism.

The close association of Buddhism with particular national cultures has also led to a readiness at times to espouse violence in defence of the Buddhist *dhamma*. In Sri Lanka and in Myanmar, members of the monastic community have been closely associated with nationalist causes, while in Japan some forms of Zen Buddhism became closely associated with martial arts and with the militaristic spirit. In Japan also, the popular Pure Land current of Buddhism was historically linked with peasant movements of armed resistance to feudal oppression, while by contrast the charismatic and prophetic figure of Nichiren insisted vehemently on the exclusive truth of his own reading of Buddhism in contrast to false teachings such as Pure Land; miraculously escaping a martyr's execution, he inspired his followers by witnessing to his faith through a harsh exile.

In the history of the various Asian countries where it has taken root, Buddhism has in general experienced only intermittent episodes of persecution. In both China and Japan it has at different times been suppressed or marginalized as a foreign cult, while in its original homeland of India it effectively disappeared for centuries, partly as a result of Muslim pressure. The most striking story of persecution today, though, is surely to be found in Tibet, where governmental policies of repression and secularization have led to an attrition of religious culture; on the other hand, the leadership and example of the Dalai Lama have proved inspirational for people of many faiths around the world.

As Buddhism is a religion where belief in God is not generally accepted, it is not really appropriate to speak of a theology of persecution in this context. However, courageous witness and restrained forbearance can surely be discerned as key elements of the spiritual response which many Buddhists would seek to make to conditions of oppression or exclusion; equally, the association in some contexts of Buddhism with a more or less aggressive resistance cannot be discounted.

vi Secularism

The meaning of the word 'secular' has changed subtly but decisively over time; as the theologian John Milbank points out, 'the secular as a domain had to be instituted or imagined, both in theory and in practice'.[19] In its original Christian use, it referred not to space but to time, the period between the Fall and the *eschaton*. With the growth of the idea that human interactions

19 John Milbank, *Theology and Social Theory*, 2nd edn (Oxford: Blackwell, 2006), p. 9.

could be understood independently of reference to God (*etsi deus no daretur*), it came to denote a political space free of theological interpretation. In states inheriting a dominant religion, it pointed to a denial of privilege to any one particular tradition. In societies marked by diversity, 'secular' was used as shorthand for processes of negotiating difference in as fair and even-handed a way as possible. In much contemporary usage, 'secularism' signifies a principled, and sometimes aggressive, resistance to what is seen as religious encroachment, particularly in the political and intellectual orders.

It is important to recognize both this range of meanings and also the emergence of a specifically secular ideological position. In its contemporary Western form, secularism cannot claim to be simply a position of neutrality among competing religious views; it is a culturally and sociologically located belief, or cluster of beliefs, commanding many people's firm adherence in much the same way as many religions do; and it can construct its own genealogy reaching back to the early modern period. Within that history and in the contemporary world, secularism, like religious beliefs, has been involved with persecution and oppression, both as victim and as agent. Our purpose in this chapter is to highlight the ways in which believers have responded to the experience of being persecuted, but we cannot ignore the extent to which those who have been victimized by religiously or ideologically justified violence can themselves become perpetrators of new cycles of violence – the terror of the French Revolution is a classic example.

That said, it is important to recognize the martyrology of those who have witnessed to secular values under conditions of oppression and persecution. Central to that witness has been a treasuring of the principle of individual freedom above any coercion or restraint imposed by powers claiming an authority derived from religion. In this sense, Nonconformist Christianity, with its emphasis on freedom to interpret the Bible, stands at the origins of the secular tradition; it was early Baptists who were among those keenest to insist on absolute freedom of religion and belief.

As the tradition developed, its narrative came to embrace also those whose freedom of thought, particularly in the sciences and arts, led them into disregard for, or denial of, Christianity in any recognizable form. This in turn led to more or less severe censure by ecclesiastical authorities, and so a roll-call of martyrs to free thought grew, including some whose primary interest was in the scientific exploration of the natural world, the artistic expression of the imagination, or the political liberation of the oppressed, as well as those who were particularly exercised by issues of belief, atheism, and ecclesiastical privilege. In our own age, there has grown up a strong, and at times perverse, insistence on the need to have untrammelled freedom not only to disagree or criticize religious beliefs or practices, but also to ridicule or insult them; thus those killed in the brutal Islamist attack on the French satirical magazine *Charlie Hebdo* were quickly enrolled as the latest martyrs of the secular tradition.

Christians experience conflicted feelings in response to this. On the one hand, as people of faith it is hurtful for us to see religious values, our own or others', denigrated and demeaned. On the other hand, subversion stands close to the heart of our faith: the Lord we follow is an enigmatic figure who was executed following accusations of both sedition and blasphemy, and the first Christians were regularly denounced as 'atheists'. Certainly if we are to find a theology, a learning from God, which will equip those of faith who are experiencing persecution, we need to have an appreciation of the strength and integrity of belief of those who, with no faith in God, experience suffering for their secular convictions.

Reflection and Response

A Theological Responses

1. Feminist, Black, Liberation, and Dalit theologies are all theological responses to categories of people being marginalized and treated unjustly, often by other Christians who have found themselves in a more powerful position. As we think of those being persecuted in the six life studies, and any other current examples, are there lessons that can be learned from these theologies?
2. In the light of this section of the chapter, are there any issues or attitudes that you wish to repent of, either for yourself or on behalf of your nation or church?

B Participating in a world shaped by many faiths and beliefs

There are certain themes that run through this overview of persecution within different faith communities, as listed below.

Persecution of other faith communities

1. What have you learned about Christianity's own history of persecuting other faiths?
2. Are there any insights here of those of a faith community persecuting others of that same faith community that relate to how Christians persecute other Christians?
3. In what way does this material change your understanding of the background to any of the life studies or other current examples of persecution?

4. How do you think that Christians should respond to other faith communities which are facing persecution?
5. Does the material raise any issues for personal or corporate repentance?

Theology of persecution and martyrdom

6. Do understandings of persecution and martyrdom within other faiths give any helpful insights into your own theological understanding of persecution and martyrdom?
7. Are there biblical passages or historical Christian examples that would relate to these theological understandings, so that you can affirm them as Christian insights?
8. There are examples of faith communities believing that God favours them and takes their side within an inter-religious dispute.

Do you think that it is appropriate for Christians to respond in this way?

9. What do you feel is God's response to those who are persecuted for their faith, both Christians and non-Christians?
10. All too often a community that was once the victim of persecution then becomes the perpetuator of persecution. How can Christians avoid doing this?

Faith, nationality, and identity

11. Are there insights to be gained about the inter-relationship between faith communities and national identity?
12. Are there insights to be gained about the inter-relationship between faith communities and being defined as being different, or 'other' than another community?

Freedom of belief

13. What are the factors that determine whether pluralism and freedom of belief are encouraged or not?
14. What are the factors that lead to either forced or insensitive conversion?
15. Why do some faiths or world-views try to convert others to their views, while others do not?
16. Why has much of secularism changed from being 'pluralistic' to being 'evangelistic'?

Reaction

17. What leads to a non-violent, violent, or holy war response at different times in a faith community's history?
18. Within Shi'a Islam, *taqiya*, or dissimulation, is seen as an appropriate response to preserve

the continuity of the faithful community. Do you think that it is an appropriate response for Christians?

C Response

1. In the light of your reflections on the material in this chapter, are there any issues or attitudes that you wish to repent of, either for yourself, or on behalf of your nation or church?
2. If possible, turn your theological conclusions from reflecting upon this chapter into prayer.

6 Worship

We have begun with prayer and so we end with worship. In between, we have considered our global context, elucidated Scripture, explored Tradition, and envisioned Reason.

When people are under pressure for their faith, they need the nourishment of worshipping their faithful God, the assurance of his presence and promises in Christ, the revivifying power of the Holy Spirit, and the knowledge that they are not alone, but are worshipping with innumerable angels and archangels and all the saints in heaven and on earth.

In our worship we:

- Praise God;
- Confess sins;
- Read and interpret God's Word;
- State our belief in God in continuity with his Church throughout the ages and the world today;
- Intercede for the needs of the world;
- Expect to meet God and be transformed by his gift of life and love in Word and Sacrament;
- Are blessed and sent out by God to work for his praise and glory.

We encourage you to respond to this theological resource by creating and using an act of worship. The responses that you have made to the previous chapters may provide you with most of the material for this; you may also wish to use some of the additional worship material that is provided below.

In doing this, it may be helpful to consider the context of a particular current example of religious persecution, either from the life studies in Chapter 2 or from a current example that you are familiar with, and have input about this early within your act of worship. If this is a corporate act of worship, you may wish to include some time for reflection upon the Scripture and the context that you are considering. These elements of worship could also be included within a service of Holy Communion.

You may wish to include some of the following elements:

- **Praise** – Some material for an opening prayer of praise may be found in your responses to Chapter 2 question D1, Chapter 3 question C1, and Chapter 4 question C1.
- **Confess** –You should have some material for this from Chapter 2 question D 2, Chapter 3 question C2, Chapter 4 question C2, and Chapter 5 question C1.

- **Hearing Scripture –** Select passages that you identified in Chapter 3 question A1 for some or all of: an Old Testament reading, a Psalm, a New Testament reading, and a Gospel reading.
- **Meeting God –** In depths of silence following hearing Scripture and receiving the Sacrament and reflecting upon your new call to action and prayer.
- **Believing –** Looking at the theological insights you have noted down and turned into prayers in response to Chapter 3 question C3, Chapter 4 question C3, and Chapter 5 question C2, write a short statement affirming your beliefs.
- **Intercede –** Write intercessions based upon the context that you are considering and other global acts of religious persecution. The Lord's Prayer should be included.
- **Being Blessed –** Receiving God's blessing and being commissioned to serve him and those

being persecuted in his world. You should have material in response to Chapter 2 question D3, and reflection on the other chapters provides additional material.

Resources

Here we provide a few resources:

Scriptures

> *Out of the depths I cry to you, O Lord.*
> *Lord, hear my voice!*
> *Let your ears be attentive*
> *to the voice of my supplications!* (Psalm 130.1–2)
> *Blessed are you when people revile you and persecute you and utter all kinds of evil against you falsely on my account.* (Matthew 5.11)
> *I am convinced that neither death, nor life, nor angels, nor rulers, nor things present, nor things to come, nor*

powers, nor height, nor depth, nor anything else in all creation, will be able to separate us from the love of God in Christ Jesus our Lord. (Romans 8.38–39)

May the God of hope fill you with all joy and peace in believing, so that you may abound in hope by the power of the Holy Spirit. (Romans 15.13)

'Worthy is the Lamb that was slaughtered
to receive power and wealth and wisdom and might and honour and glory and blessing!' (Revelation 5.12)

The one who testifies to these things says, 'Surely I am coming soon.'
Amen. Come, Lord Jesus! (Revelation 22.20)

Prayers

The Jesus Prayer

Lord Jesus Christ,
Son of God,
have mercy on me,
a sinner.

Agnus Dei

Lamb of God,
you take away the sin of the world,
have mercy on us.
Lamb of God,
you take away the sin of the world,
have mercy on us.
Lamb of God,
you take away the sin of the world,
grant us your peace.

Prayer of St Chrysostom

Almighty God, who hast given us grace at this time with one accord to make our common supplications unto thee; and dost promise that when two or three are gathered together in thy Name thou wilt grant their requests: Fulfil now, O Lord, the desires and petitions of thy servants, as may be most expedient for them; granting us in this world knowledge of thy truth, and in the world to come life everlasting. Amen.

The Lord's Prayer (Matthew 6:9 13)

Our Father in heaven,

hallowed be your name.

Your kingdom come.

Your will be done,

on earth as it is in heaven.

Give us this day our daily bread.

And forgive us our debts,

as we also have forgiven our debtors.

And do not bring us to the time of trial,

but rescue us from the evil one.

The Litany (The Book of Common Prayer)

That it may please thee to forgive our enemies, persecutors, and slanderers, and to turn their hearts.

Blessing

Now to him who is able to keep you from falling, and to make you stand without blemish in the presence of his glory with rejoicing, to the only God our Saviour, through Jesus Christ our Lord, be glory, majesty, power, and authority, before all time and now and for ever. Amen. (Jude 24–25)